GUIDE FOR C
SUNDAY MASS

PAUL TURNER

Nihil Obstat
Rev. Mr. Daniel G. Welter, JCD
Chancellor
Archdiocese of Chicago
October 5, 2018

Imprimatur
Most Rev. Ronald A. Hicks
Vicar General
Archdiocese of Chicago
October 5, 2018

The *Nihil Obstat* and *Imprimatur* are declarations that the material is free from doctrinal or moral error, and thus is granted permission to publish in accordance with c. 827. No legal responsibility is assumed by the grant of this permission. No implication is contained herein that those who have granted the *Nihil Obstat* and *Imprimatur* agree with the content, opinions, or statements expressed.

This book is part of the Preparing Parish Worship™ series.

This book was edited by Danielle A. Noe, MDiv. Michael A. Dodd was the production editor, Anna Manhart was the series designer, and Juan Alberto Castillo was the cover designer and production artist.

23 22 21 20 19 1 2 3 4 5

Printed in the United States of America

Library of Congress Control Number: 2018965358

ISBN 978-1-61671-487-1

EGCSM

CONTENTS

PREFACE

Salome brushed the dining area clean, arranged the table, cleared room for everyone to recline, and turned her attention to the fire.

"Don't touch," she scolded her curious daughter. "You'll get burned."

Lifting a tray of fish, Salome pushed it into the oven. Simon and John nodded at each other. Today's catch had been unusually large. Overcome with joy that Simon had seen the Risen Lord that same day, they anticipated celebrating his Resurrection with a fitting banquet.

Martha and Jude burst into the room, breathless from running. Before they could get a word out, John shared the good news: "The Lord has truly been raised and has appeared to Simon!"[1]

Martha and Jude responded together with similar good news: "We have seen the Lord!"

"I thought you went to Emmaus," said Salome.

"We did," responded Martha. "But on our way a stranger joined us, asked about the events here in Jerusalem, and then corrected our impressions when he opened the scriptures to us. We pressed him to stay for dinner, and when he took the bread and broke it, we realized that this was no stranger."[2]

"It was Jesus," crowed Jude, "risen from the dead!"

"Peace be with you."[3] A voice suddenly came from nowhere. Simon and John glanced around the door. Salome looked behind the oven. Then, in the far corner

1. Luke 24:34.
2. See Luke 24:13–32.
3. Luke 24:36.

of the room they saw a figure. "It's a ghost!" said Salome's daughter, hiding behind her mother. Martha shrieked. Jude positioned himself in front to protect her.

"Why are you troubled?" the figure asked, "And why do questions arise in your hearts?"[4]

Salome's lips were quivering. A gradual realization came over her like the uncovering of an ancient secret. "It's . . . It's . . . It can't be."

"Look at my hands and my feet, that it is I myself,"[5] said the figure. Jude started to approach him, but then turned back to Martha. The figure seemed to laugh at this. "Touch me and see, because a ghost does not have flesh and bones as you see I have."[6] He stepped closer to the fire, and the flames illumined his limbs.

John, still traumatized by the crucifixion of his mentor, was looking down. He saw the marks of the nails in the figure's feet, then the hands stretching out toward him, marked the same way.[7]

Jubilation filled the room as together they recognized the stranger in their midst: Jesus, risen from the dead.

"Have you anything here to eat?" he asked.[8]

"Have we what?" asked Simon, amazed at this unexpected question.

"Everyone, please," said Salome. "Recline at the table." They took their places as she opened the oven and pulled out the fish. She offered it first to the visitor.[9] Jesus took a piece "and ate it in front of them."[10]

He said to them, "These are my words that I spoke to you while I was still with you, that everything written about me in the law of Moses and in the prophets and psalms must be fulfilled."[11]

He explained the Scriptures. He showed how from ages past the prophets foresaw that the Messiah would suffer as he did—this they had seen. And that he would rise as he did—this they now witnessed.

Simon was overcome with joy and purpose. "We have to tell the world."

---

4. Luke 24:38.
5. Luke 24:39.
6. Luke 24:39.
7. See Luke 24:40.
8. Luke 24:41.
9. See Luke 24:42.
10. Luke 24:43.
11. Luke 24:44.

"And you will," said Jesus. "You are witnesses. You will receive power, and you will preach not only these events, but also repentance and forgiveness. Start here in Jerusalem. Then tell all the nations."[12]

After these encounters, the disciples continued to gather to commemorate the Resurrection on the day they called "the Lord's Day." They often ate fish. But they always broke bread and shared a cup. They did this in memory of Jesus. At his request, they did not stop speaking when the meal was over. They bore witness to him, and they preached his message to the world.

12. See Luke 24:46–49.

WELCOME

In memory of Jesus, Catholics gather on the Lord's Day to celebrate Mass. We dedicate time. We leave home. We gather with friends and strangers. We enact a predictable ritual, and we change in unpredictable ways. We place all the events of the past week inside that Mass to offer them for the glory of God. We prepare for the duties of the coming week and seek their sanctification. We discard from our lives what keeps us from Christ, and we retain what makes us good disciples.

On the night before he died, Jesus reclined at table with his disciples. He declared that the bread was his Body, the wine his Blood. He sacrificed himself for the disciples he loved. After that day, every time they ate and drank, they proclaimed his death. They did this in memory of Jesus. And so do we.

Welcome to *Guide for Celebrating Sunday Mass.* By using this book along with the primary ritual books (such as The Roman Missal and the Lectionary for Mass) and liturgical documents (such as the General Instruction of the Roman Missal), you will be able to prepare and celebrate the most important ceremony in the Catholic liturgy. The centerpiece of all Catholic piety, the Mass is the memorial of the sacrifice of Jesus Christ, the sharing of the eucharistic meal, and a foretaste of the banquet in the age to come.

In addition, the Mass is the most ordinary experience of Catholic communal prayer. It brings the community together to strengthen their identity as the Body of Christ. It provides a place for them to bring the fruits of their faithful witness, and it prepares them to go into the world to proclaim the Gospel, inviting others to follow Christ.

This book will equip those who prepare Sunday Mass to understand its overall structure, individual parts, and meaning. It presents a history of development while exploring the contemporary Sunday celebration.

You will find answers to frequently asked questions, and a resource list and glossary, which will invite you to go deeper into understanding.

Throughout, this book will help you participate better when you are at Mass, and to give you the tools to let others share your experience and even go beyond. Your sacred gathering may then mutually enrich your faith and prepare you to celebrate one day the eternal supper of the Lamb of God.

About the Author

Paul Turner is pastor of the Cathedral of the Immaculate Conception in Kansas City, Missouri, and director of the Office of Divine Worship for the Diocese of Kansas City–St. Joseph. He holds a doctorate in sacred theology from Sant'Anselmo in Rome. His publications include *At the Supper of the Lamb* (Chicago: Liturgy Training Publications, 2011), *Glory in the Cross* (Collegeville, MN: Liturgical Press, 2011), and *Celebrating Initiation: A Guide for Priests* (Chicago: World Library Publications, 2008). He is a former president of the North American Academy of Liturgy, a member of *Societas Liturgica*, and the Catholic Academy of Liturgy. He is a recipient of the Jubilate Deo Award (National Association of Pastoral Musicians) and the Frederick McManus Award (Federation of Diocesan Liturgical Commissions). He serves as a facilitator for the International Commission on English in the Liturgy and as the ecumenical officer for the Diocese of Kansas City–St. Joseph. He enjoys the Kansas City Symphony and the Kansas City Royals.

The Theological and Historical Developments of the Sunday Mass

"For the Christian, Sunday is above all an Easter celebration, wholly illumined by the glory of the Risen Christ."

—*Dies Domini*, 8

Sunday Mass is the cornerstone of Catholic spirituality. Catholics perform other admirable activities. They teach, they feed the hungry, they visit the sick, they pray. Nonetheless, participating at Mass is the center of all these activities.

For Catholics, the principal attraction to Sunday Mass is the real presence of Christ in the Eucharist. According to Jesus' own words, we believe that something extraordinary happens to the bread and wine at Mass. Many believers pay special attention when the priest repeats Jesus' words from the Last Supper: "This is my Body." "This is my Blood." That moment at Mass stands out from all the rest.

> The liturgy is the summit toward which the activity of the Church is directed; at the same time it is the fount from which all the Church's power flows.
>
> —*Constitution on the Sacred Liturgy*, 10

For similar reasons, Catholics also show respect to the tabernacle, which houses previously consecrated eucharistic bread. We believe that Christ is truly present in this Blessed Sacrament housed in the tabernacle. Wherever the tabernacle is located in the church, it invites us to adore Christ.

Yet Jesus asked us to do something more: to eat his Body and drink his Blood. When we do, we do not merely adore him. We share life with him. He lives in us.

The Mass is more than a personal encounter with Christ, as riveting as that is. Much more than an occasion for personal adoration, the Mass gathers the faithful as the Body of Christ, giving thanks and offering sacrifice to the Father. At church, we meet others who share our values. We give and receive support. We keep in touch with friends. We connect with strangers. We meet Christ individually, but we also meet his Body, the Church.

Together, this body of the faithful raises a common voice in prayer. The people express their unity by assuming common postures and exchanging mutual gestures. Even though we all experience some disagreements within the community, our faith in Christ firmly holds us as one.

> Through this bread there comes about what we see in the gospel: a fellowship of pilgrims, a fellowship gathered around the apostles, a fellowship of a meal that includes everyone, a fellowship of one single pilgrim path to God.
>
> —Karl Rahner

Mass reaches its climax when the gathered participants share the Body and Blood of Christ in Communion. The unity of the faithful with one another and with Christ is revealed and enriched.

This communion follows sacrifice. We offer to God the efforts we have made to spread the Gospel throughout the previous week. We contribute to the support of the parish. We accept the inconvenience of going to church and the petty annoyances that distract us while we are there. We offer ourselves in sacrifice to God, and we share divine life in Communion.

The ceremony is repetitious. Many words and gestures do not change. Yet repetition helps Catholics enter the Paschal Mystery more deeply. Freed from the challenge to create new prayer every week, the entire community can focus on the matter at hand. Outside of the liturgy, many individuals follow a daily routine that involves hygiene, news, meals, work, study, and play. These habits help them accomplish tasks and feel at peace. The same applies to liturgical prayer. The difference is that liturgical prayer shapes what we believe and how we should act.

The Lord's Day is the first day of the week. It commemorates the day that Jesus Christ rose from the dead. By setting aside Sunday as a day of worship, Catholics profess their faith in the Resurrection. When they share in the Sacrament of Holy Communion, they eat and drink the Body and Blood of the Risen Christ. We observe the Lord's Day differently from other days. Even the rest we take on Sundays foreshadows the eternal rest to which Christ invites us.

The Lord's Day was the day that the New Testament associated with the breaking of bread.[1] This practice derived from early testimony concerning the Last Supper. All four evangelists describe a meal on the night before Jesus died, but Matthew,[2] Mark[3] and Luke[4] especially present the details of Jesus' words and actions with bread and wine, with which Catholics have become so familiar.

> At Sunday Mass, Christians relive with particular intensity the experience of the apostles on the evening of Easter when the Risen Lord appeared to them as they were gathered together.
>
> —*Dies Domini,* 33; see John 20:19

Many may not realize, however, that the earliest evidence for the Last Supper comes from Paul's first Letter to the Corinthians.[5] The stories of Jesus' life were probably shared orally for several decades before they were written down as Gospel accounts near the end of the first century. But Paul's letters date to the middle of that century. Even then, he says that he is passing on what he received from the Lord. He testifies that the first Christians were already gathering for the Eucharist in fulfillment of Jesus' command, "Do this in remembrance of me."[6]

Sunday became the preferred day. Even though the Last Supper probably took place on a Thursday, the Mass does not commemorate that meal, but the entire mystery of the passion, death, and Resurrection of Christ. The weekly Sunday observance of the Resurrection thus became the perfect platform for celebrating the real presence of the Risen Christ in the Eucharist.

The Second Vatican Council's *Constitution on the Sacred Liturgy* expressed this beautifully:

At the Last Supper, on the night when he was betrayed, our Savior instituted the eucharistic sacrifice of his body and blood. He did this in order to perpetuate the sacrifice of the cross throughout the centuries until he should

1. For a more scholarly treatment of the origins of the Eucharist sketched below, see Barry Craig, *Fractio panis: A History of the Breaking of Bread in the Roman Rite*. Studia Anselmiana (Rome: EOS-Editions of Sankt Ottilien, 2011); Paul F. Bradshaw and Maxwell E. Johnson, *The Eucharistic Liturgies: Their Evolution and Interpretation* (Collegeville, MN: Liturgical Press, 2012); and Paul F. Bradshaw, "Did Jesus Institute the Eucharist at the Last Supper?" in *Issues in Eucharistic Praying in East and West: Essays in Liturgical and Theological Analysis*, ed. Maxwell E. Johnson (Collegeville, MN: Liturgical Press, 2010), p. 12.
2. See Matthew 26:26–30.
3. See Mark 14:22–26.
4. See Luke 22:17–20.
5. See 1 Corinthians 11:23–26.
6. 1 Corinthians 11:24.

Sunday is the preferred day for remembering the Paschal Mystery of Christ.

come again and in this way to entrust to his beloved Bride, the Church, a memorial of his death and resurrection: a sacrament of love, a sign of unity, a bond of charity, a paschal banquet "in which Christ is eaten, the heart is filled with grace, and a pledge of future glory given to us."[7]

Thus, the sacrifice of Calvary was anticipated at the Last Supper within a memorial that Jesus entrusted to the Church for the future. We call that memorial the Mass.

The origins of the Catholic Mass lie in an activity that the apostolic Church called the breaking of bread. All references to this title come from Luke, both in the post-resurrection account of his Gospel and in his second volume, the Acts of the Apostles.

In all, Luke makes six references to the breaking of bread. In the Gospel, on the night of the Resurrection, Jesus appeared to two disciples, who recognized him "in the breaking of the bread."[8] The second chapter of Acts of the Apostles has two references. On Pentecost, filled with the Holy Spirit, Peter gave an exhortation to the crowd, and three thousand stepped forward for Baptism. These first converts "devoted themselves to the teaching of the apostles and to the communal life, to the breaking of the bread and to the prayers."[9] Similar testimony appears a few verses later: "Every day they devoted themselves to meeting together in the temple area and to breaking bread in their homes. They ate their meals with exultation and sincerity of heart, praising God and enjoying favor with all the people."[10] Their numbers increased.

Later in Acts, Luke says that Paul held a discussion "on the first day of the week, when we gathered to break bread."[11] At one point, Paul went "upstairs, broke the bread, and ate; after a long conversation that lasted until daybreak, he departed."[12] Still later, on board ship amid a storm at sea, Paul

7. *Constitution on the Sacred Liturgy* (CSL), 47.
8. Luke 24:35; see also Luke 24:30.
9. Acts of the Apostles 2:42.
10. Acts of the Apostles 2:46–47.
11. Acts of the Apostles 20:7.
12. Acts of the Apostles 20:11.

"took bread, gave thanks to God in front of them all, broke it, and began to eat."[13] It is not clear if all of these directly refer to a celebration of the Eucharist, but the repetition of the phrase shows that the expression had entered the vocabulary and practice of the first Christians.

Wine is not mentioned in any of these passages. "Breaking bread" probably became shorthand for the entire meal, which would naturally have included wine and other foodstuffs. The meal took place regularly on the first day of the week.

In other sources, not only is wine mentioned, but it is mentioned first. Just before describing the Last Supper in his first Letter to the Corinthians, Paul wrote, "The cup of blessing that we bless, is it not a participation in the blood of Christ? The bread that we break, is it not a participation in the body of Christ?"[14] There is other evidence for the cup-bread sequence, [15] though it did not endure. Early Christian communities did not all celebrate the Eucharist the same way.

> The cup of blessing that we bless, is it not a participation in the blood of Christ? The bread that we break, is it not a participation in the body of Christ? Because the loaf of bread is one, we, though many, are one body, for we all partake of the one loaf.
>
> —1 Corinthians 10:16–17

Paul also extolled unity: "Because the loaf of bread is one, we, though many, are one body, for we all partake of the one loaf."[16] From the beginning, the celebration of the Eucharist was never isolated from Christian unity, identity, and behavior.

The breaking of bread likely became one way in which the community expressed its new pattern of calling upon God through Jesus[17] or in Jesus' name.[18] Prayer was also offered to "the God and Father of our Lord Jesus Christ."[19] There is also prayer to God and Jesus[20] and to Jesus alone.[21] These various threads gradually wove the fabric that became the Christian celebration of the Eucharist.

13. Acts of the Apostles 27:35.
14. 1 Corinthians 10:16.
15. See, for example, Luke 22:7–20.
16. 1 Corinthians 10:17.
17. See, for example, Romans 1:8.
18. See, for example, John 16:23–24.
19. 2 Corinthians 1:3; Ephesians 1:3; Colossians 1:3.
20. See, for example, 1 Thessalonians 3:11–13.
21. See, for example, 2 Corinthians 12:8-9; Acts of the Apostles 7:59–60.

The celebration of the Eucharist is never isolated from Christian unity, identity, and behavior.

In time, the words that today's Catholics associate with the consecration ("This is my body; this is my blood") became a central feature of eucharistic praying at the breaking of the bread. However, it was not always that way. John did not include them in his Gospel account of the Last Supper. None of the evangelists considered these words significant enough to record them in Jesus' own language, Aramaic, for the sake of precision, as was the case with less neuralgic words such as "*Raqa*,"[22] "*Eli, Eli, lema sabachthani*,"[23] "*Talitha cum*,"[24] "*Ephphatha*,"[25] "*Abba*,"[26] and "*Rabbouni*."[27] Perhaps at the beginning, the connection between the Last Supper and the eucharistic meal was self-evident.

The first Christian converts from Judaism probably gathered for the Eucharist using meal prayer patterns with which they were familiar. At the time of Jesus, pious Jews offered prayers before and after meals. The blessing of food after the meal, the *birkat ha-mazon*, probably influenced the Christian breaking of bread. Unfortunately, sample prayers contemporaneous with Jesus are unknown today. A tenth-century manuscript includes a blessing or praise of the God who nourishes, followed by a thanksgiving for the land and food, and a prayer for Jerusalem. Later eucharistic prayers imitated this pattern: first praise, then petition.

Christian prayer built on this Jewish precedent. The clearest example is the *Didache*, a manual for orderly life in the Church. Possibly compiled near the end of the first century, it is contemporaneous with the late New Testament books. Chapters 9 and 10 concern meal prayers, and these are commonly thought to supply the roots of Christian eucharistic praying.

The *Didache* includes elements of thanksgiving for the cup and the bread, a petition for the gathering of the Church, and the limitation of

22. Matthew 5:22.
23. Matthew 27:46 and Mark 15:34.
24. Mark 5:41.
25. Mark 7:34.
26. Mark 14:36.
27. John 20:16.

participation in the Eucharist to those who have been baptized. Chapter 9 opens with thanksgiving over the cup and the bread—in that order. It recalls the sequence found in 1 Corinthians 10:16–17 and Luke 22:7–20, strengthening the idea that some early Christians shared the cup before the bread.

Ignatius of Antioch (+117) referred to the Eucharist as "breaking one loaf."[28] By participating in it, people looked beyond death to eternal life in Jesus Christ. Ignatius is perhaps best known for comparing his impending martyrdom to the making of bread. He considered himself God's wheat, ground by the teeth of wild beasts, that he might be found pure bread in Christ.

> We give you thanks, our Father, for the life and knowledge which you made known to us through Jesus your Child. To you be glory for ever.
>
> —*Didache,* Prayer over the Bread

Polycarp was martyred about the same time, though the acts of his martyrdom date to the third century. His dying prayer resembles a eucharistic prayer: he praises God for giving him a share in the cup of Christ, and then prays that God will accept the sacrifice of his life. Martyrs physically imitated the sacrifice of Christ, as those who shared the Eucharist did sacramentally.

The earliest developed description of a Eucharist comes from Justin Martyr (+165). His account reads remarkably similar to present-day celebrations.[29] He teaches that the bread and wine are the flesh and Blood of Christ, and that they become so through the giving of thanks and a word of prayer. He also records the eucharistic words of Jesus, and he refers to the Gospel accounts as his source.

Irenaeus (+202) explains the significance of the practice of giving thanks or celebrating "Eucharist."[30] God needs nothing from us; the offering is made for the purposes of thanksgiving and sanctifying. Not all the early sources report that a minister repeated the eucharistic words of Jesus from the Last Supper. Irenaeus is among those who implied that he did. Interestingly, he treats first the Blood and then broken bread.

28. *Letter to the Ephesians*, 20.
29. See *Catechism of the Catholic Church* (CCC), 1345.
30. *Against the Heresies* 4:18,16.

Tertullian (+220) describes Jesus taking bread and giving it to the disciples while saying, "This is my body," and he links the cup with the covenant sealed by Jesus' Blood.[31]

More eucharistic allusions come from apocryphal sources dating to the same period. These claimed authorship by the Apostles and their contemporaries, but scholarship dates them to the first couple of centuries after the completion of the New Testament. They helpfully represent trends in worship shortly after the period that they claim to represent. Among these early references to the breaking of bread, the *Gospel according to the Hebrews* (end of the first and early part of the second centuries) says that Jesus took bread and offered a blessing, and then broke and gave it.[32] The *Acts of John* (second century) assigns the same actions to the apostle.[33] The prayer that John offers resembles those of the *Didache*. *The Acts of (Judas) Thomas* (third century) tells of several celebrations of the Eucharist, only two explicitly mentioning both a loaf and a cup. One account has a prayer addressed to Jesus that begins, "Your holy body which was crucified for us we eat."[34] It also says that the community drinks the Blood poured out for them for salvation. This is the first reference from the early Church that links the bread and wine with the crucified Body and Blood of Christ, though it does not otherwise recount the events of the Last Supper. Furthermore, the prayers in this source are invocations, not thanksgivings, showing another stage of development.

The *Didascalia apostolorum* (c. 240) includes traces of eucharistic praying. A variety of practices still prevailed, including one option for a guest bishop to preside only over the prayer concerning the chalice. The same source encourages people to "pray and offer for those who are fallen asleep."[35] This may show the link between the Eucharist and the martyrdom of Christians. Prayer for the dead eventually became common in eucharistic prayers, but it first appears only in the age of the martyrs.

The eucharistic prayer of Addai and Mari has ancient origins, perhaps in the mid-third century. It is still used today in the Eastern Catholic Chaldean Rite, headquartered in Baghdad. Even today, it does not include the most famous words of Jesus, "This is my body. This is my blood." In 2001, the

31. *Against Marcion* 4:40, 3.

32. Cited by St. Jerome, *On Famous Men*, 2.

33. 85–86 and 109–110.

34. Craig, p. 95.

35. Bradshaw and Johnson, pp. 56–57, citing *Didascalia* 6.22 from Vasey and Brock, *The Liturgical Portions of the Didascalia*, 33.

Vatican's Pontifical Council for Promoting Christian Unity together with two other congregations published an agreement that the eucharistic prayer of Addai and Mari is valid for the celebration of the Eucharist "from a historical, liturgical and theological perspective."[36] The agreement was surprising because the Roman Rite considers the words of institution essential for the consecration of the bread and wine, but not surprising given the antiquity of this eucharistic prayer and the context in which it developed. It came from a Church that focused more on the breaking of bread, a celebration of unity that looked forward to the eternal banquet.

Texts from the third century are the first references linking the crucified Body and Blood of Christ to the bread and wine.

In the period between the Resurrection of Jesus and the end of the third century, then, the Eucharist was administered in a variety of locations by different groups under varying authorities. There was no overall consensus about how to celebrate the rite. People acted according to local needs and inherited tradition. Groups of disciples and individual theologians shared the best practices with which they were familiar. It took a while for the Mass to take the shape we know today.

By the third and fourth centuries, two eucharistic prayers gained widespread usage, both of which became important later in the Roman Catholic Church. St. Ambrose of Milan gave the earliest testimony for a eucharistic prayer that he knew from the Christians in Rome. It went through considerable development later, especially in the Middle Ages. When the first Roman Missal was published in 1475, it became the only eucharistic prayer in force. Hence, it was the "canon"—the one way of doing things. And it was "Roman" because of its origins. The Roman Canon was the only eucharistic prayer in use for many centuries; today it is also known as Eucharistic Prayer I.

Eucharistic Prayer II is based on a prayer in the *Apostolic Tradition* from the same period. It also has a Roman connection. Over time, it had been lost and was rediscovered only in the nineteenth century. After the Second Vatican

36. *Guidelines for Admission to the Eucharist Between the Chaldean Church and the Assyrian Church of the East*, 3; available from www.vatican.va/roman_curia/pontifical_councils/chrstuni/documents/rc_pc_chrstuni_doc_20011025_chiesa-caldea-assira_en.html; accessed May 14, 2018.

Council, when the Catholic Church approved an expanded number of eucharistic prayers, the committee working on the Order of Mass unanimously accepted the addition of this prayer. That committee considerably emended it to fit modern sensibilities, and it has become one of the most popular eucharistic prayers of the Catholic Mass.

The Mass underwent many more developments. By the seventh century the Gelasian Sacramentary, compiled in a religious community outside Paris, had organized sets of presidential prayers: the collect, the prayer over the offerings, and the prayer after communion. Prefaces and blessings were all under development at the same time. Many of the prayers that Catholics hear at Mass today repeat these ancient texts preserved for many centuries.

Some of the dialogues of the Mass can be traced to the third and fourth centuries, such as the one that opens the eucharistic prayer. Both the *Apostolic Tradition* and the *Apostolic Constitutions* show evidence of the complete preface dialogue that Catholics know well today. The universal prayer (prayer of the faithful) has its origins in the same period; it fell out of use for many centuries, however, and was restored after the Second Vatican Council.

The Second Vatican Council called for a revision of the liturgical books and a restoration of ancient liturgical practices.

Variation in the prayers and ceremonies had continued, but these became more regularized after the tenth century with the compilation of the Roman-Germanic Pontifical. The Roman Missal of 1475 strengthened the growing centralization of eucharistic practice. Its revision in 1570 made it the standard prayer book for the Roman Catholic Mass for five centuries, undergoing a number of relatively minor adjustments along the way. The Second Vatican Council authorized a new edition of the same Missal, employing sources recently discovered, rearranging the material, and simplifying some parts of the celebration in order to express a refined eucharistic and ecclesial theology. The Council called for the full, conscious, active participation of the people, which they expressed as baptized members of a royal priesthood, thanking God, offering sacrifice, and sharing communion. This participation opened up the dynamics of the Catholic Mass.

The Council also authorized a revised Lectionary. The earliest centuries of Christian worship provide only sketchy evidence for the readings assigned to various days. A list of readings had been compiled in the fifth century Wurzburg Lectionary. There can be found, for example, a reading for Palm Sunday that is still proclaimed today as the second reading for the same day. The 1570 Missal included readings for the entire liturgical year and other occasions. Typically, the priest proclaimed two readings at each Mass: an epistle and a Gospel. There were very few readings from the Old Testament in the 1570 Missal. One of the greatest achievements of the conciliar liturgical reform was the 1969 *Lectionary for Mass*, which provides three readings plus a responsorial psalm for every Sunday Mass and solemnity, arranged on a three-year cycle. Whereas on weekdays in the 1570 Missal the priest usually proclaimed the readings from the previous Sunday, the post-conciliar Lectionary provides a rich two-year cycle of readings for weekdays for Ordinary Time. The revised Missal also diversified the ministries, making it more customary now for lay readers and ideally a deacon to proclaim the readings, not the priest.

> The Church earnestly desires that all the faithful be led to that full, conscious, and active participation in liturgical celebrations called for by the very nature of the liturgy. Such participation by the Christian people as "a chosen race, a royal priesthood, a holy nation, God's own people" (1 Peter 2:9; see 2:4 – 5) is their right and duty by reason of their baptism.
>
> —*Constitution on the Sacred Liturgy*, 14

Participating at Sunday Mass is the most important act that Catholics do. It brings the previous week to a conclusion. It sets the following week on the right path. Through it we offer all the sacrifice of our work and our love. The Mass invites us to communion with one another and with Christ. It sends us into the world to bring Christ and to be Christ.

Most importantly we gather to share the Eucharist because on the night before he died, just before accepting his cross, anticipating the mystery of the Resurrection, Jesus asked us to do this. We are his disciples. We obey his will. We do this in memory of him.

Preparing the Sunday Mass

"On the first day of each week, which is known as the Day of the Lord or the Lord's Day, the Church, by an apostolic tradition that draws its origin from the very day of the Resurrection of Christ, celebrates the Paschal Mystery. Hence, Sunday must be considered the primordial feast day."

—*Universal Norms on the Liturgical Year and the General Roman Calendar*, 4

Everyone who participates in the Sunday Eucharist prepares for it. The priest and deacon review their parts and vest accordingly.[37] The preacher meditates on the Scriptures and other parts of the day's celebration to prepare a homily. Musicians have selected pieces and practiced them.

Readers have become familiar with their readings. Ushers and greeters have dressed accordingly and arrived at church in due time. Extraordinary ministers of Holy Communion have arranged their schedules to be present to serve.[38] Those responsible for the decorations and liturgical environment have spent time preparing and arranging the appearance of the church inside and out. A worship team has evaluated past experiences and prayerfully prepared what they hope will inspire all participants. And every person who comes to church has prepared to enter into the mystery of the Eucharist through a life of service and sacrifice, by setting aside time for worship, and arriving at church in time to prepare their minds and hearts for the mysteries about to unfold. Everyone prepares for Mass.[39]

The greatest care is to be taken that those forms and elements [of the liturgy] proposed by the Church are chosen and arranged, which . . . more effectively foster active and full participation and more aptly respond to the spiritual needs of the faithful.

—*General Instruction of the Roman Missal*, 20

37. See *General Instruction of the Roman Missal* (GIRM), 335–347 and *Redemptionis sacramentum* (RS), 121–128 regarding proper ministerial vesture (priests, deacons, and lay ministers).

38. See *Norms for the Distribution and Reception of Holy Communion* (NDRHC), 28 and RS, 154–160.

39. See GIRM, 91–94 concerning the duties and ministries involved in the Mass; GIRM, 95–97 regarding the role of the people of God; and GIRM, 98–111 regarding particular ministries.

Those most responsible for the ceremonies should become familiar with the basic liturgical books.

The Roman Missal includes the prayers that the priest says aloud, as well as the ceremonial instructions (the rubrics). It embraces both the everyday words and actions as well as the specific prayers and ceremonies assigned to particular days. The first pages present the *General Instruction on the Roman Missal* (GIRM), which gives a theological and practical overview for the Mass. Although it is dense, it is the go-to document for understanding what we do and why.

The Missal then turns to the Proper of Time. These pages span the entire liturgical year from beginning to end, and they supply the antiphons and prayers assigned to each day. The entrance and communion antiphons may be replaced with congregational hymns, and they often are. The presidential prayers that appear on each page belong to the priest. He offers the collect, the prayer over the offerings, and the prayer after communion at every Mass, while the people pray along with him in silence. On some days the Proper of Time includes a specific preface to open the eucharistic prayer.

All who prepare the liturgy must become familiar with the liturgical books and governing Church documents.

The Order of Mass occupies the middle of the Missal, easily findable because of the tabs that reach out from its pages. This is the basic script of a typical Mass—the dialogues, acclamations, prayers, and rubrics that remain consistent at every Mass throughout the year. The Order of Mass includes dozens of prefaces from which the priest may choose, depending on the nature of the celebration.

The Proper of Saints offers the prayers and antiphons specific to certain calendar days when saints are commemorated and celebrated. The Commons that follow this section come into use when the community celebrates a saint or occasion for which the Missal may not have specific texts.

The Ritual Masses include the prayers for special celebrations, such as baptisms and weddings. The Masses for Various Needs and Occasions supply prayers for both church and civic needs—texts for every occasion from the election of the pope to the aversion of winter storms.

The main body of the Missal closes with Votive Masses pertaining to certain devotions observed by the faithful and Masses for the Dead providing prayers for funerals or celebrations in remembrance of the deceased.

The Lectionary is arranged in four volumes. The first includes the readings for Sunday Mass according to their three-year cycle. Volumes II and III provide the readings for weekday celebrations. In Ordinary Time the first reading and responsorial psalm are spread over a two-year cycle. Volume II contains Year 1, and Volume III contains Year 2. Volume IV contains all the readings that may be used for other observances—Baptisms, weddings, and funerals, as well as many of the other celebrations included in the Missal. A slim Lectionary supplement was published in 2017 to add readings needed for updates to the liturgical calendar and practice.

The *Book of the Gospels* is just that—a book that arranges the Sunday Gospel readings for the year. The first volume of the Lectionary includes everything that the *Book of the Gospels* contains, but this special book plays an important role in processions and proclamation because it features the words of Christ.

The *Book of the Gospels* is the only ritual book that is elevated and carried in procession.

Other ritual books may be used on Sunday: The *Rite of Baptism for Children* or the *Rite of Christian Initiation of Adults*, for example. The *Book of Blessings* also includes many prayers that may be incorporated into the celebration of Sunday Mass, such as the commissioning of new extraordinary ministers of Holy Communion.[40]

Before Mass begins, other preparations need to be made. Someone should write the petitions for the universal prayer (prayer of the faithful). If the priest or deacon or another minister makes announcements at the end of the service, these too require preparation.

The church will be decorated according to the time of year or celebration at hand. During Advent a wreath may be prominently displayed, and the violet colors worn by the principal ministers may be repeated in

40. Those who prepare the liturgy should also familiarize themselves with the various liturgical documents of the Church. Refer to the resources section on page 88 for a list of the primary documents.

decorative tones. At Christmas Time, many churches erect a manger in an area where people may direct their attention before or after Mass. In Lent a bare church will give a sense that even the building is fasting. Easter Time presents the best opportunity for festive decoration. Throughout Ordinary Time, when ministers wear green vesture, the liturgical environment can enhance the community's prayer in various ways.

> Special care must be taken to ensure that the liturgical books, particularly the *Book of the Gospels* and the Lectionary, which are intended for the proclamation of the Word of God and hence receive special veneration, are to be in a liturgical action truly signs and symbols of higher realities and hence should be truly worthy, dignified, and beautiful.
>
> —*General Instruction of the Roman Missal,* 349

Many people find the ordo a helpful tool in preparing liturgies. Published every year and regionally, the ordo contains information about the particular celebrations assigned for each day. If you are wondering when Ash Wednesday falls, when diocesan days of prayer are assigned, when the anniversary of the dedication of your cathedral is to be observed in parishes, and when Advent begins, the ordo has it all figured out year by year. Occasionally the Vatican adds a celebration to the liturgical calendar. Until the liturgical books are updated, these can be found in the ordo.[41]

The liturgical calendar ranks celebrations in this order: solemnities, feasts, and memorials. Some memorials are optional, but the others are to be observed. Days without such ranks are ferial, the weekdays that require no specific observance. Those are the weekdays when votive Masses or Masses for various needs and occasions may be celebrated. Liturgical colors are linked to liturgical days.

The two main divisions of the Mass are the Liturgy of the Word and the Liturgy of the Eucharist. Two other parts bracket these: the Introductory Rites and the Concluding Rites. The Introductory Rites gather the community and invite us to prepare individually and as a group for all that will follow. The Concluding Rites sum up all that has preceded and sends us forth, strengthened by the Word and Sacrament to live as Christ's disciples in the world.[42]

41. Those who prepare the liturgy should also review *Universal Norms on the Liturgical Year and the General Calendar*, the Vatican document on the liturgical year. It is found in the third edition of *The Roman Missal.*

42. See GIRM, 27–28.

Arriving

Before the Mass can begin, the people have to arrive. The Introductory Rites open with these words: "When the people are gathered." As people arrive at church, they will naturally greet others on the way in. Some parishes station greeters at the doors to ensure that all who arrive receive a friendly welcome. Everyone can contribute to this atmosphere if they arrive early enough to greet other worshippers—even those they have not yet met. This very human action fosters a sense of community that will underlie participation throughout the entire liturgy.

As a devotional practice, Catholics dip their fingers into holy water as they enter the church and make the sign of the cross over their forehead, breast, and shoulders. They are reminding themselves of their Baptism.

Upon entering the nave, people take the seat of their choice. Some look for places in the back of the church or in an unoccupied pew. However, every single person will be participating at this Mass. Each person will invest in the community's prayer if they select a place near the front.

No rules govern how an individual prepares to celebrate the Mass, and parishioners do so in a variety of ways.

Before people enter a pew, they genuflect to the tabernacle by lowering one knee to the ground as a sign of reverence for the Real Presence of Christ in the Blessed Sacrament.[43] Many Catholics make the sign of the cross while they do this, but it is not necessary. Some hold the pew to balance themselves. It's fine. The direction of the genuflection is not toward the altar or the cross, but toward the tabernacle.[44]

In some churches, the tabernacle is outside the main worship space. In that case, people make a low bow toward the altar before taking their place. The altar is the

43. See GIRM, 314–317.
44. See GIRM, 273, 274–275 and BLS, 70–80.

central focus of the Mass. It represents Christ and it is the place where the memorial of his sacrifice will take place.[45]

Many Catholics make the sign of the cross when they enter the pew and kneel down for a few moments of private prayer before the Mass begins. No rules govern this action, but the custom helps them prepare for what follows. They may think about the particular concerns that fill their minds today. They may recite favorite prayers. They may think back over the past week or anticipate the activities to come. Or they may just try to empty their minds completely so that the Holy Spirit may enter. In these few moments worshipers exercise their prayer muscles, much as athletes stretch before performing.

Other uses for this time before Mass sometimes vie for attention. Some members engage in lively chatter. Others prefer silence for prayer. The choir or organist may offer a prelude. The cantor may rehearse congregational music. Worshippers are entitled to some silence before the service begins, but they can best prepare for their responsibilities during the Mass by thinking charitably of all those concerned with other activities.

The Introductory Rites

The first part of the Mass is called the Introductory Rites. These are all of the rites that precede the Liturgy of the Word, including the opening procession, the greeting, the penitential act or sprinkling, the Gloria, and the collect. The purpose of these rites is to "ensure that the faithful, who come together as one, establish communion and dispose themselves properly to listen to the Word of God and to celebrate the Eucharist worthily."[46]

Entrance Chant

All may sing an opening song together. In Masses without music for this moment, someone—or everyone—reads the words of the entrance chant assigned to that day in *The Roman Missal*. If you are selecting music for the entrance chant, be sure to check the entrance antiphon for a suggestion. Many people choose music that pertains to the readings or the season, but another

45. See GIRM, 296–308; RS, 129–131; and BLS, 56–60.

46. GIRM, 46; see also GIRM, 120–127, 172–174, 188–189, 194–195, 210–211 and *Sing to the Lord: Music in Divine Worship* (STL), 139–141. In some cases, such as the Rite of Acceptance into the Order of Catechumens, the regular celebration of the Introductory Rites is omitted (see GIRM, 46).

worthy option is a song inspired by the words in the antiphon of the day.

This song enhances the unity of all who sing it. It also starts them thinking about the reason they have gathered on this day. The entrance chant accompanies the procession of the ministers. It appropriately concludes shortly after the presider reaches his chair.[47] However, sometimes, for the integrity of the text being sung, it may extend a little longer.

The entrance song opens the celebration and enhances the unity of all who sing it.

Some individuals consider themselves poor singers, but the church expects participation now and during other sung parts of the Mass. When the songleader invites people to turn to a certain page, they should pick up the worship aid and find the music. "God dwells within each human person, in the place where music takes its source."[48] People can pray more fully when they sing.

Individuals who do not sing may actually hinder the unity that the song is designed to create. A person who does not sing may appear disinterested to other worshippers, making their task more difficult. This is especially true of ministers visible to others in the congregation. They above all lead by example when they sing. Participation will inspire others. Encourage people to pick up the songbook, even to mouth the words in rhythm and think about their meaning. They will praise God as they prepare themselves and the whole community to celebrate Mass.[49]

For the entrance procession, servers lead the way. If incense is used, the thurifer enters at the head of the procession, followed by the cross bearer and

47. See GIRM, 310 and BLS, 63–65 regarding the presidential chair.
48. STL, 1.
49. See GIRM, 47–48, 121 and RS, 57 and STL, 142–144.

candle bearers.[50] If this cross is to become the main cross of the Mass, it must bear an image of the crucified Christ; otherwise, a bare cross is acceptable.[51] The deacon carries the *Book of the Gospels* to be placed on the altar. In his absence, a reader carries this book.[52] The *General Instruction of the Roman Missal* says that the minister "places" it on the altar, which seems to imply laying it flat, in imitation of the tradition in the Eastern Rites.[53]

> Great importance should therefore be attached to the use of singing in the celebration of Mass, with due consideration for the culture of peoples and abilities of each liturgical assembly.
>
> —*General Instruction of the Roman Missal,* 40

The priest enters last. Ministers genuflect to the tabernacle if it is in the sanctuary; otherwise, the genuflection is omitted. They reverence the altar by making a low bow. The priest and deacon kiss its top. Both the *Book of the Gospels* and the altar represent Christ. The two are juxtaposed at the beginning of the Mass, symbols of the presence of Christ in the upcoming Liturgy of the Word and the Liturgy of the Eucharist.[54]

Sign of the Cross

The priest says the words to the sign of the cross as he and other worshippers touch their own forehead, breast, and shoulders. As the priest concludes, the people answer "Amen." This simple gesture places everything that follows under the cross of Jesus Christ. As Jesus sacrificed himself on the cross for our sakes, so he invites us to sacrifice our lives for the sake of the Gospel. Throughout this liturgy we pray to the Father, through the Son, and in the Holy Spirit. From the beginning, we celebrate Mass in the name of the Trinity.

Catholics frequently use the sign of the cross to begin and end prayer, especially at mealtime. By making the cross a part of daily life, Catholics will add meaning to this gesture as the Mass gets underway.[55]

---

50. See GIRM, 276–277 and BLS, 92–93.
51. See BLS, 91.
52. See GIRM, 120.
53. See GIRM 173 and 195.
54. See GIRM, 49–50 and 122–23.
55. See GIRM, 50 and 124.

Greeting

The priest greets the people with a biblical formula such as "The Lord be with you" (other options are found in the Missal). He prays that the Lord will be present among the gathered people. The people express much the same sentiment in their response "And with your spirit." St. Paul concludes several of his letters with a prayer that the Lord will be with the spirit of the people reading his message. This initial greeting invites all into the presence of the living Christ. A secular greeting, such as "Good morning," is not used. It may seem polite to say, but it would usurp the force of this short dialogue. Two brief phrases establish the roles of the priest and the people. The greeting puts them in conversation with each other, and it begs for the presence of Christ now and throughout this time of common worship.[56]

In the Penitential Act, we ask Christ to have mercy on us.

The priest may then say a few words of introduction to the Mass. He may speak about some of the groups at church today or about the season or feast being celebrated. Up to this point the priest has spoken official formulas of the Church's liturgy to open the celebration, but here he may use his own words.[57]

Penitential Act

The priest invites all to acknowledge their sins before God. They have entered a holy place and a holy time. God made us, loves us, and remains faithful to us, but all of us fail our side of the covenant. We approach this Mass with humility and honesty. All is not lost: In acknowledging our sins, we experience God's mercy.

This invitation opens the first of several opportunities for communal silence during the Mass.[58] Participants fill this silence by privately

56. See GIRM, 50 and 124.

57. See GIRM, 50.

58. "Sacred silence also, as part of the celebration, is to be observed at the designated times. Its nature, however, depends on the moment when it occurs in the different parts of the celebration. For in the Penitential Act and again after the invitation to pray, individuals recollect themselves; whereas after a reading or after the Homily, all meditate briefly on what they have heard; then after

acknowledging their own sinfulness. Other silences have different purposes, but they all draw the community together into common participation.

There are different forms of the penitential act. Often the priest leads the Confiteor, in which all present confess their sins to one another and to God. Acknowledging their faults, all strike the breast once, imitating the gesture of the penitent tax collector in Luke 18:13. We also ask God, the saints, and the others present to pray for us.

Or, the priest leads the people in a brief dialogue that begs God's mercy and salvation. These words come mainly from the Book of Psalms, and they have been part of the Introductory Rites of the Mass for many centuries.

Following either of these first two forms of the penitential act is the Kyrie, a brief litany in which we ask Christ the Lord to have mercy on us. By asking for Christ's mercy, we profess that he has the power to forgive and the desire to achieve reconciliation for us.[59]

The liturgical greeting invites all gathered into the presence of the living Christ.

In another version of the penitential act, the priest, deacon, or another minister (perhaps a cantor) incorporates this litany to Christ into a series of invocations. These praise the greatness of Christ and plead for his mercy. The three invocations focus not upon how sinful we are, but upon how merciful Christ is. These may be drawn from the Missal's appendix, from the previous translation, or from original creations. If you are composing these, be sure to focus on Christ ("You came to call sinners. Lord, have mercy") and not on the people ("We have sinned against you. Lord, have mercy.")[60]

Communion, they praise God in their hearts and pray to him. Even before the celebration itself, it is a praiseworthy practice for silence to be observed in the church, in the sacristy, in the vesting room, and in adjacent areas, so that all may dispose themselves to carry out the sacred celebration in a devout and fitting manner" (GIRM, 45).

59. See STL, 146.

60. See GIRM, 51–52, 125 and STL, 145–146.

Blessing and Sprinkling of Water

On Sundays, in place of the penitential act, the priest may lead the blessing and sprinkling of water. In this ritual we call to mind our Baptism and enter the celebration of Mass with a heart made pure. During Easter Time, the priest may be blessing water that has already been blessed—just as every Mass concludes with a blessing of people who have already been blessed. The priest may then walk through the church, sprinkling blessed water upon the members of the gathered assembly. Traditionally, he uses a metal sprinkler (aspergillum), but some priests use a branch or a brush. Meanwhile, the assembly sings a song about the water. This music is different from the entrance song that precedes it and from the Gloria that usually follows it.[61]

Gloria

On most Sundays and on solemnities and feasts of the year, everyone sings the Gloria. Like the entrance chant, it joins the community's voices into a hymn of praise. Unlike the entrance chant, its words are always the same, and they address both the Father and the Son with the Holy Spirit.

The Gloria has a celebratory feel to it, even though it includes petitions for Christ's mercy. We do not sing the Gloria during Advent and Lent because of the preparatory and penitential nature of those seasons, and to help the celebrations of the rest of the year stand out in stronger relief.

As a hymn, the Gloria has a celebratory form, and it is best practice for it to be sung, although it may be recited.

If people do not sing it, they may all recite the Gloria. Still, it is a hymn, and its nature is to be sung. Some musical settings incorporate a congregational refrain. These are useful when the people have difficulty learning a complete Gloria without a refrain, or for one-time regional celebrations that gather people from different parishes who may not all share the same

61. See STL, 147.

repertoire of music. However it is presented, the Gloria should sound as though everyone is praising God in unison.[62]

Collect

The priest says, "Let us pray." After those three words, he should leave some time of silence so that all may actually pray. The silence has a purpose. People are not just waiting for the server to carry the Missal to the priest, or for the priest to find the correct page. The silence is for each worshipper. We use it to become aware of God's presence. If people have practiced prayer at home during the week, this will not be difficult. They put themselves again in the presence of God. In addition, the silence is a good time for worshippers to call to mind any intentions they bring to this Mass. After the priest says "Let us pray," people are not just waiting for the next words. They are actively participating, sharing silence with others, filling the time with a sense of God's presence, and formulating the intentions closest to their heart. The server can help this effort by presenting the book to the priest *before* the words "Let us pray."

The priest collects all the prayers of all the people gathered for this Mass, and he summarizes them in the collect. Each Sunday he offers a specific prayer that the Church has assigned for that day. Catholics at Mass all over the world hear the same Collect. Some of these prayers are over a thousand years old. Others were composed in the late 1960s. They all try to articulate the needs of the people unified for this celebration and present them humbly and convincingly before God.

A typical collect has several parts. As an example, here is a breakdown of the one for the Fourteenth Sunday in Ordinary Time. The priest uses direct address to call upon God by some title ("O God"). The priest then recalls something that God has done in the past ("who in the abasement of your Son have raised up a fallen world"). The priest then makes a specific petition ("fill your faithful with holy joy"), and

"Let us pray" is a call for the assembly silence. The text that follows "collects" the prayers of the people.

62. See GIRM, 53, 126 and STL, 148–150.

then he suggests why this is a good idea ("for on those you have rescued from slavery to sin you bestow eternal gladness.") As in this example, the words flow in a way that puts a climactic idea at the end of the sentence.

You may use a similar argument when you ask a neighbor for help. "John, you've been so good to me every time I needed something that I hate to ask again, but could I borrow your lawnmower so that I can get my property to look as nice as yours?"

If people listen carefully to each collect, they will be able to join with the priest in prayer. The central part of any collect is the petition. We're asking God to do something. As individuals reflect upon the presence of God and the specific intentions they bring to this Mass, they can place all these intentions into the hands of the priest, who puts them before God on their behalf. In the example above, the priest is asking that we all be filled with holy joy, especially those whom the worshipers have called to mind during the silence that follows the words "Let us pray."

Following the collect, children may be dismissed for their own Liturgy of the Word in a room where they hear Scriptures and a homily at their level of understanding. In this case, someone—perhaps the deacon if there is one, or a priest if there is not—invites the children to form a procession. A catechist accompanies them, perhaps carrying the *Lectionary for Masses with Children*. The person dismissing the children invites them to a listen carefully to God's Word, and to return after the Universal Prayer for the Liturgy of the Eucharist.[63]

In many parishes, children of ages four to nine are dismissed after the Collect to hear the Scriptures and a homily or reflection on the Word adapted to their level of understanding.

The collect concludes the Introductory Rites. Throughout this part of the Mass we have gathered as one, exchanged greetings, acknowledged our sins, and praised the God of mercy. We have also called to mind the needs that have cried for attention. It is time for the first major division of the Mass, the Liturgy of the Word. All are seated.[64]

63. See the *Directory for Masses with Children* (DMC), 17 and 19.

64. See GIRM, 54, 127 and STL, 151.

The Liturgy of the Word

The Bible is the Word of God. It is a living word. The Bible does not simply possess a record of things that God said and did in the past. It is one way that God continues to speak to us. In fact, when the Scriptures are proclaimed during the Mass, you are hearing the Word of God, speaking out loud, alive in your community today.

Catholics have a reputation for not knowing the Bible very well, but we probably know it better than many people realize. The prayers we hear at Mass are intricately entwined with Biblical references. As with other Christian churches, our hymns refer to passages from the Scriptures. Most importantly, we highlight the proclamation of the Word of God at every Mass. If you go to Mass regularly, you will hear all the most important passages of the Bible arranged in a way to aid your appreciation of them. These readings are distributed in a series of books we call the *Lectionary for Mass*.[65]

The Readings

At a typical Sunday Mass people will hear a passage from the Old Testament, they will join in singing a responsorial psalm, they will hear a second reading from one of the New Testament letters, and then a climactic passage from one of the Gospel accounts. During Easter Time the rirst reading comes from the Acts of the Apostles, and some of the second readings come from the Book of Revelation.[66]

> When the Sacred Scriptures are read in the Church, God himself speaks to his people, and Christ, present in his word, proclaims the Gospel.
>
> —*General Instruction of the Roman Missal,* 29

The Sunday readings are arranged on a three-year cycle. Year A features Gospel readings from Matthew, Year B from Mark, and Year C from Luke. Excerpts from John's account are proclaimed in all three years of the cycle, especially during Lent and Easter, but occasionally in Christmas Time and Ordinary Time.

During Ordinary Time the first readings leap through the Old Testament to find passages that link with themes from the Gospel. For example, sometimes characters in the stories bear similarities, or a prophecy in the first

65. See GIRM, 55.
66. See GIRM, 57–65, 128–138, 175–177, 212–213 and RS, 61–63 and STL, 152–154.

reading is fulfilled in the Gospel. The second readings in Ordinary Time string together several passages from one New Testament letter for several weeks at a time. For example, you'll hear excerpts from St. Paul's Letter to the Romans in Year A, from Ephesians in Year B, and from Galatians during Year C. Paul's first Letter to the Corinthians is so important and so long that Ordinary Time begins in January each year with several weeks of readings from this letter every year of the cycle.

The Sunday readings are arranged in a three-year cycle.

The Responsorial Psalm generally relates to the theme shared by the Gospel and the First reading, although there are exceptions. In rare occasions it makes an allusion to the second reading. During the periods of Advent, Christmas Time, Lent, and Easter Time, a psalm sometimes fits the time of year rather than a specific reading. At times the psalm is replaced with a canticle from the Old or New Testament. A canticle is a song that resembles a psalm but is found in a different book of the Bible. Because the psalm was composed as a song, singing it fulfills its design.[67]

In Advent the first readings are prophecies about the coming of Christ, and the second readings show how the first Christians looked forward to his glorious return. The Gospel of the First Sunday of Advent always anticipates the Second Coming of Christ. The Gospel accounts on the Second and Third Sundays tell about John the Baptist. The Gospel on the Fourth Sunday reports some of the events leading up to the birth of Jesus. During Christmas Time all the readings combine to reflect on the mystery of the Incarnation.

In Lent the Old Testament readings summarize important events from salvation history. The First Sunday presents something from the first chapters of the Bible. The Second Sunday tells of Abraham, while the Third Sunday moves the story to Moses. The Fourth Sunday tells of later developments—from entering the Promised Land to exile from it. On the Fifth Sunday we hear the words of one of the prophets. Throughout this time the second readings generally take up a theme either from the first reading or the Gospel.

67. See STL, 155–160.

> The Responsorial Psalm . . . is an integral part of the Liturgy of the Word and . . . has great liturgical and pastoral importance, since it fosters meditation on the Word of God.
>
> —*General Instruction of the Roman Missal,* 61

The Gospel accounts on the first two Sundays of Lent always tell of Jesus' temptation in the desert and his Transfiguration on the mountain. In Year A, the Gospel accounts for the next three Sundays are specially chosen to accompany the elect on their journey towards Baptism: the woman at the well, the man born blind, and the raising of Lazarus. All three stories come from John. They proclaim how people came to a deeper faith in Christ, as those approaching Baptism still do today. The Gospel accounts on the same Sundays in Year C focus rather on those who are already Christians, who keep Lent as a time of renewal: Jesus cursing the fig tree, the parable of the prodigal son, and the forgiveness of the adulterous woman. They explore the mystery of sin, repentance, and forgiveness. Year B's Gospel accounts on these weeks prepare the entire community for the coming days of the Passion: Jesus cleansing the Temple, Nicodemus coming to faith, and the parable of the grain of wheat that dies in order to rise. All these episodes point the way toward the cross.

The readings for Palm Sunday, Holy Week, and Easter Sunday all focus on the particular days at hand.

In Easter Time the first readings from Acts of the Apostles tell how the first Christian community grew. These accounts provide a source of inspiration especially for the newly baptized. The second readings in Year A come from the first Letter of Peter, which has strong baptismal themes, and Year B offers the first Letter of John, which tells of the early Church community. The second readings from Year C, taken from Revelation, acclaim the glory of Christ.

The Gospel on the Octave of Easter (the first week of Easter) is the same every year. John tells us what happened on the Sunday following the first Easter Sunday: Jesus returned to reveal himself again to the Apostles, this time with the formerly absent Thomas. The Gospel accounts of the Third Sunday recount another appearance of Jesus after the Resurrection. On the next several Sundays the Gospel comes from John's account of the farewell discourse, the final instructions that Jesus gave the Apostles at the Last Supper, and from the prayer he offered the Father on the same occasion. The readings for Pentecost all explore the themes of that solemnity.[68]

Before the proclamation of the Gospel, the cantor may intone the Gospel acclamation and sing a verse. During most of the year, the acclamation is "Alleluia," but during Lent we use a different acclamation in praise of Christ and his Word. This continues a longstanding custom that the word *Alleluia* not be spoken or sung during Lent. The Church "fasts" from this joyful shout until it is solemnly proclaimed—in a sense reborn—at the Easter Vigil. Throughout Easter the liturgy brims with Alleluias.[69]

On great solemnities of the Church, the Gospel procession may be more elaborate.

During the Gospel acclamation a procession forms. All who have been seated now stand. If incense is used, it is prepared.[70] If there is a deacon, he asks the priest for a blessing. Sometimes the deacon or the priest simply walks from his chair to the ambo, but on many occasions ministers who carry incense and candles lead the procession, while the deacon or the priest carries the *Book of the Gospels*. Ideally, the music for the acclamation covers this entire procession. All of this draws attention to the significance of the proclamation about to happen, in which words about Christ—and indeed words from the lips of Christ—are to be heard.[71]

Adding to the solemnity of the Gospel, the deacon or priest who proclaims it greets the people: "The Lord be with you." As he announces which of the four Gospel accounts supplied this passage, he uses his thumb to trace the sign of the cross on the book, and then upon his own forehead, lips, and heart. Meanwhile, all others imitate him, making the sign of the cross over their own forehead, lips, and heart. No words accompany this gesture, but it seems intended to prepare us to listen to Gospel with an alert mind, bold lips, and a loving heart.

68. See STL, 167–169.
69. See STL, 161–164.
70. See GIRM, 276–277.
71. See GIRM, 132–134.

If incense is used, the deacon or priest then takes the thurible from the server and incenses the Book of the Gospels. That server and the ones holding candles may remain in place for the entire proclamation of the Gospel. All of them face the ambo as a sign of reverence.[72]

A short acclamation concludes each of the readings. After the first and second readings, all say, "Thanks be to God." In the acclamation that concludes the Gospel, people address Jesus Christ. He has just spoken his Word to the community today, and all acknowledge that they are even now experiencing his presence: "Praise to you, Lord Jesus Christ."[73]

The Ambo

The readings are all proclaimed at the ambo. Although it resembles a lectern or pulpit, it has a specific purpose associated with the Word of God. In addition to the readings, the responsorial psalm may be sung from there. Its verses come directly from the Bible, so it functions as another reading of Sacred Scripture. The homily may be preached from the ambo. The petitions in the universal prayer (the prayer of the faithful) may come from the ambo as well. At the Easter Vigil, the Exsultet is proclaimed from the ambo. Otherwise, it should not be used. Song leading and announcements take place in some other location. The ambo is sacred space because of the sacredness of the Word of God.[74]

It is preferred practice that the readings, including the Responsorial Psalm, and the Universal Prayer take place from the ambo.

The Sequence

On Easter Sunday and Pentecost Sunday all sing or recite the sequence after the second reading. The sequence is a hymn that expresses the themes of a particular day. On two other occasions (the Solemnity of the Most Holy Body and Blood of Christ and the Memorial of Our Lady of Sorrows), the

72. See GIRM, 133 and 276–277.
73. See GIRM, 128.
74. See GIRM, 309 and *Built of Living Stones* (BLS), 61–62.

sequence is optional. Because its words are found in the Lectionary, it could be led from the ambo. However, the sequence properly belongs to the entire assembly, so the song leader could cue the people from the cantor stand.[75]

Listening to the Word of God

Before coming to Mass, people would benefit from praying over the upcoming readings at home. The assigned passages can be found in many printed and online resources. Many people like to read along at Mass as the reader, deacon, or priest proclaims the readings. Many believe that they can better follow the content this way, especially if the amplification is poor, if the reader has not prepared well, or if the person hearing the reading more regularly uses a different language. Undeniably, there are benefits to reading along at Mass. However, something else is happening at the moment that a reading is being proclaimed. The Word of God is sounding in the church. God's Word is spoken aloud. It sounds anew today. If people just use their ears to hear the Word, they will hear it as it is meant to be—the voice of God speaking right now. If you are ever present for Mass where the entire community listens together without reading along, you will experience something very special. When all ears are open to the Word of God, the Word resounds powerfully in the room. It demands the listening participation of all the people.

> The Gospel, radiant with the glory of Christ's cross, constantly invites us to rejoice.
>
> —*Evangelii gaudium*, 5

Preparing to Hear the Word of God

You may encourage people to prepare to hear the readings in their daily prayer. They may read a passage before mealtime or make the readings part of their morning prayer before going to church. Worshippers will gain a sharper appreciation of the readings if they devote time to them at home before listening to them at church. They will hear different nuances from the reader (who may be instituted or a lay person),[76] and they will be prepared to hear how the homilist approaches the same passages.

75. See STL, 165–166.
76. See GIRM, 196.

The Homily

After the proclamation of the Gospel, all sit for the homily. Normally the presider preaches, but he may pass the responsibility to another priest or to a deacon. By its nature, a homily is preached by an ordained minister. Reflections by lay people may take place during announcements near the end of Mass, or in non-eucharistic settings, or as brief summaries in a language that the homilist did not use.[77] The homily usually draws its theme from the readings of the day, especially the Gospel. However, the priest or deacon may preach about some other part of the Mass—the collect, the eucharistic prayer, or the entrance chant, for example.[78]

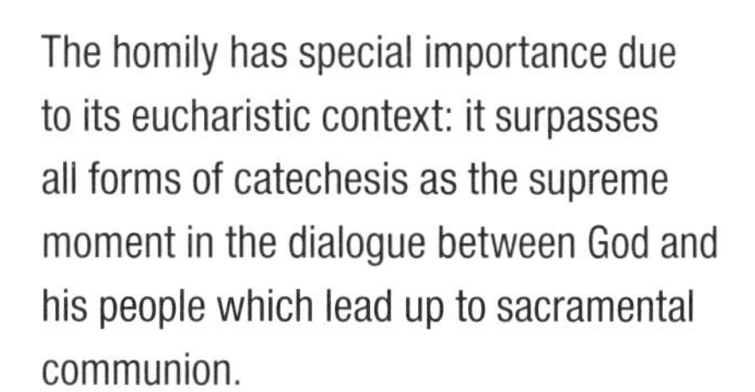
The homily has special importance due to its eucharistic context: it surpasses all forms of catechesis as the supreme moment in the dialogue between God and his people which lead up to sacramental communion.

—*Evangelii gaudium*, 137

Dismissal of Catechumens

When catechumens are present, they may be kindly dismissed after the homily. Catechumens are unbaptized adults or children of catechetical age in formation for their initiation. Those in their final weeks of preparation are called "the elect." Catechumens are not required to leave after the homily; they are allowed to remain for the Liturgy of the Eucharist. However, an old tradition calls for their dismissal.

Most parishes that retain the practice dismiss catechumens into a session that forms their faith; that is, the catechumens leave the Mass, but they go to another room where they reflect on the readings, learn more about their faith, and practice it together.

Another reason for their dismissal is that catechumens are not yet equipped to participate fully in the rest of the Mass. Only the baptized are able to profess the creed, offer the prayer of the faithful as adopted children of God, exchange the Christian peace, and share Holy Communion. Catechumens are dismissed not only because they lack formation, but because they have not yet been baptized into the priestly people of God.[79]

---

77. See RS, 74.
78. See GIRM, 65–66, 136, 213 and RS, 64–68 and 161.
79. See the *Rite of Christian Initiation of Adults* (RCIA), 67, 75.3, 83.2, and 120, D.

Other Ceremonies

On some occasions, an additional ceremony follows the homily; for example, the Baptism of a child, Confirmation, Matrimony, Ordination, or a prebaptismal rite for adults.[80]

The Creed

On Sundays and solemnities throughout the year, all the faithful stand to proclaim the creed. Normally they recite the Nicene Creed, but the Apostles' Creed may substitute. For example, the Church recommends, but does not require, that the Apostles' Creed be professed during Lent and Easter. The Apostles' Creed resembles the baptismal promises, which everyone renews at the Easter Vigil, and it enlivens the spirit of apostolic faith throughout Easter Time. It may be sung or said.[81]

With the creed, each person assents to the common faith that draws this community together, a faith shared by Christians throughout the world. When worshippers come to the words about the conception and birth of Christ, they make a low bow in the direction of the altar, humbling themselves before him who humbled himself to become one of us. Church councils have recognized these creeds as an accurate summary of principal Christian beliefs since the early days of Christianity.[82]

Universal Prayer or Prayer of the Faithful

The universal prayer brings the Liturgy of the Word to its close. Also called the prayer of the faithful, it calls upon the baptized members of the community to exercise their priestly ministry by praying for the needs of the Church and the world. The priest introduces this part of the Mass, but the intentions are to be named by the deacon, the reader, or another minister—not by the priest. If a deacon is present, he usually presents the petitions,[83] but another person could do so because

> The people respond in some sense to the Word of God which they have received in faith and, exercising the office of their baptismal Priesthood, offer prayers to God for the salvation of all.
>
> —*General Instruction of the Roman Missal*, 69

80. Advice for integrating these into the liturgy follows later in this book beginning on page 55.
81. See STL, 170.
82. See GIRM, 67–68, 137 and RS, 69.
83. See GIRM, 177.

The Universal Prayer calls upon the baptized members of the community to exercise their priestly ministry by praying for the needs of the Church and the world.

this part of the Mass is not restricted to an ordained minister. The petitioner is speaking to the people, telling them what intention needs prayer—for example, "That our Church may embrace the challenge to evangelize, let us pray to the Lord." Then the people pray to God, using a formula such as "Lord, hear our prayer."

The intentions may be composed in each parish. They should appeal to God on behalf of the Church, public authorities and the salvation of the world, those burdened with difficulties, and the local community. Often these prayers include a petition for the sick and the dead. Sometimes the petitions include a specific intention for which a donor has offered a stipend to the priest.

Coming after the dismissal of catechumens, the universal prayer is an exercise of those who share the common priesthood of Jesus Christ by means of their Baptism. The Church relies on baptized members to concentrate on these petitions. They share in the common priesthood of Jesus Christ. Therefore, they pray.

All have been standing for the universal prayer because they have actively been addressing God. Afterwards, the congregation sits.[84]

If children were dismissed for their own Liturgy of the Word, they return to the main assembly after the universal prayer.

The Liturgy of the Word highlights the proclamation of readings from the Bible. The readings are proclaimed without interruption or commentary so that the community may hear just the Word of God. The Liturgy of the Word then includes preaching and prayers. All of it is centered on the ambo, the table of God's holy Word.

84. See GIRM, 69–71, 138, 177, 197–198 and STL, 171.

The Liturgy of the Eucharist

The second main part of the Mass is the Liturgy of the Eucharist, during which the faithful present their gifts to God and join with the priest in giving thanks for all God's blessings. During the eucharistic prayer they witness the consecration of the bread and wine into the Body and Blood of Christ and become present to the offering that Jesus made of his own life on Calvary. They call upon God as their own Father and share the fruits of this offering—Communion in the Body and Blood of Christ.[85]

The Preparation of the Gifts

For bread, many Catholic churches use hosts that workers in religious houses have specially baked for Mass. Such communities have the equipment that fittingly processes wheat flour and water. Some people are gluten intolerant, so the Catholic Church permits the use of low-gluten hosts. Those who cannot even tolerate that product may receive Communion from the cup, so parishes should be ready to offer that option. Those who cannot tolerate alcohol can request permission from the bishop to receive Communion under the form of mustum, a grape juice in which fermentation is stopped shortly after it begins. As parish leaders get to know the names and circumstances of parishioners, they will be better positioned to address these special needs. A regular feature on the website or in the bulletin will share the news with visitors searching for a place that can accommodate their health concerns.[86]

> It is a praiseworthy practice for the bread and wine to be presented by the faithful.
>
> —*General Instruction of the Roman Missal*, 73

Some parishes bake their own bread, and they are limited to the ingredients of wheat-flour and water. The results are not always as tasty as the hosts produced by retailers. Still, one disadvantage to small hosts is that they minimize the symbol of the breaking of bread, one of the features that express the unity of the people gathered in communion. Bread "must be recently made" and "have the appearance of food."[87]

85. See GIRM, 72–89, 139–165, 178–183, 190–193, 214–215 and NDRHC, 26.
86. See GIRM, 319–324 and RS, 48–50 regarding the requirements for the bread and wine.
87. GIRM, 320–321.

Many grains of wheat form one loaf. The wheat is ground into flour; each grain gives up its appearance in service to the flour. The flour is mixed with water; each Christian has been baptized for a common purpose. The dough has been baked in heat; Christians are tried by the fire of spiritual struggles, in order to become more worthy exemplars of the Body of Christ.

Many grapes form one flask of wine. The grapes are ground into juice; each grape gives up its appearance in service to the liquid. The liquid is fermented; Christians are steeped in the gifts of the Holy Spirit. Wine brings joy and flavor to those who drink it; Christians bring the joy of the Gospel to the waiting world.

These are the elements that Jesus took at the Last Supper. He pronounced the bread and wine to be his Body and Blood. He asked the disciples to do this in memory of him. Obedient to his command, we present bread and wine so that the Holy Spirit may change them for us into the Body and Blood of Christ, and that we might be transformed into better instruments of his service.

Before the bread and wine are brought to the sanctuary, ushers usually take up a collection of monetary offerings from those participating in this Mass. The collection accomplishes the practical function of helping the parish pay its bills, but its significance is far deeper. Together with the bread and wine, the collection indicates the willingness of God's people to sacrifice themselves for the sake of the Gospel. It is one way that they participate in the self-offering of Jesus Christ.

The collection indicates our willingness to sacrifice ourselves for the sake of the Gospel.

Because we tend to protect our money, many of us contribute sparingly to the Sunday collection. But the collection is one sign of how committed we are to Christ. When we give generously and gladly, we imitate the sacrifice of Jesus Christ. In a sense, contributing to the collection is a privilege within the Church. Catechumens may be dismissed before this point, not because they have not yet received contribution envelopes, but because only the baptized members of the Body of Christ can fully offer themselves in union with Christ. Our gifts to the Church show our commitment to Christ.

Traditionally, the Church recommends a tithe (ten percent of one's income) to charities. If people contribute five percent of their income to their parish church, and another five percent to other causes, they are probably doing their part. However, some people can do more, and they should, for the sake of the Gospel.

All may be invited to join in singing a hymn. Each Mass has an offertory chant that may be sung or omitted. Unfortunately, the words that the liturgy has assigned to each Mass are not very accessible. Omitted from the Missal, they appear in the *Graduale Romanum* and the *Graduale Simplex*—books that very few parishes own. The assigned chant traditionally features a verse from the Bible. The words may or may not relate to the action underway or the Scriptures of the day. The recommended text may be replaced by another sacred song, and almost always is. Singing at this time is another opportunity to engage the active participation of the people.[88]

Singing the offertory hymn is another important way to engage the active participation of the people in the Mass.

The servers, the deacon, and the priest prepare the altar. Up to this moment, the action of the Mass has taken place elsewhere—at the chair from which the priest presides, or at the ambo where the readings are proclaimed. Now the focus moves to the altar.

To begin, a corporal is unfolded on top of the altar. This square white cloth designates the area on which the offerings of the people will be placed. It is the symbolic destination of the offering that the faithful make of themselves to God.[89]

Other vessels may be brought to the altar—for example, extra chalices for the wine that will be consecrated and shared in the community. The cloths used to wipe the rims of the chalices at Communion time, the purificators, may be laid next to the vessels. If the priest uses a chalice veil, it will be removed at this time. If he uses a pall,

88. See STL, 173–175.

89. See GIRM, 140–144.

a stiff square that sits on top of a chalice to protect the wine from insects, it may be brought to the altar as well.[90]

The gifts of bread and wine are presented next. Members of the faithful may bring them forward up the aisle through the assembly. They may carry the collection basket as well, which will sit on the floor or a table apart from the altar. All these gifts are entrusted to the priest for his prayers. He is gathering everyone's sacrifice and placing it symbolically on the altar.[91]

The ideal is that "the faithful" bring forward the gifts. Sometimes people want to involve children too young to receive Communion or non-Catholic spouses. This gives them something to do at Mass. However, those who present the gifts are ideally among those who will be receiving back the same bread and wine consecrated as the Body and Blood of Christ. Their sacrifice leads to their communion.

> Sacred vessels should be made from precious metal. If they are made from metal that rusts or from a metal less precious than gold, they should generally be gilded on the inside.
>
> —*General Instruction of the Roman Missal,* 328

The deacon or the priest adds a little water to the wine. This practice probably originated in days when strong wine needed to be diluted. Today this gesture has become a symbol of the Incarnation of Jesus, who "mixed" his divinity with our humanity. The minister prays that Christ share his divinity with us humble humans through our participation in the Eucharist.

The priest leads a prayer to God, whose goodness has provided the bread and wine being offered. If he says the prayer out loud, all respond, "Blessed be God for ever." At times, he says the prayers quietly, especially if people are singing a hymn. After praising God for these gifts, the priest places them onto the corporal. Once called "gifts," they are now called "offerings" because they have been designated to share in the sacrifice of the Mass.

The priest bows down before the altar to say a quiet prayer. He is asking that we may all be acceptable to God, that our sacrifice may be pleasing. The prayer is based on one from the prophet Daniel. Three young men in a fiery furnace pray that God will be pleased with the sacrifice of their lives. The

90. See GIRM, 327–324 and RS, 117–120. Note that in the dioceses of the United States, "sacred vessels may also be made from other solid materials which in the common estimation in each region are considered precious or noble, for example, ebony or other harder woods, provided that such materials are suitable for sacred use" (GIRM, 329).

91. See RS, 70.

When the faithful bring up the gifts of bread and wine, it is symbolic of the entire community's sacrifice that is offered to God.

priest is praying that God will accept all the sacrifices represented on the altar, including his and yours.

The priest may incense the offerings.[92] No words accompany this action, but he continues to show the connection between the gifts of the people and the sacrifice of the Mass. After the offerings, he incenses the cross, the symbol of the death of Christ, whose sacrifice is commemorated in this sacred meal. He then incenses the altar, which also symbolizes Christ our cornerstone, and which serves both as the altar of sacrifice and the table of Communion. He incenses in order that the sweet aroma of these offerings may please God. Then, because we are all offering ourselves as well, a minister incenses the priest and the people. It is customary for people to stand for the incensation, copying the posture of the priest. Even though many priests and people bow back to the server when the server bows to them, the GIRM requires only that the server bow.[93] The server is not exchanging pleasantries with the priest and the people; the server is honoring them with incense. The smoke unites all of us as we symbolically place ourselves upon the altar with the bread and wine as offerings to God. Perfumed by the smoke, we hope that God will be attracted to the smell of our lives and service.[94]

Servers help the priest wash his hands. This practice probably began as a practical matter following the use of incense. Now it has become a final act of purification before the priest begins the eucharistic prayer. He asks God to forgive his sins so that his prayer on behalf of the people wil be worthier.[95]

The priest invites everyone to join his prayer that God will be pleased with these sacrifices. The people stand to express their desire that God will accept the sacrifices for two purposes—for the praise of God's name, and for the good of the Church.[96]

---

92. See GIRM, 276–277.
93. See GIRM, 277.
94. See GIRM, 144.
95. See GIRM, 145.
96. See GIRM, 146.

Finally, the priest leads the prayer over the offerings. This prayer changes from day to day. Like the collect, the Church assigns a particular prayer each Sunday so that all priests all over the world say the same one each week. Also like the collect, some of these prayers are more than 1500 years old; others are remarkably new. In the prayer over the offerings the priest expresses the common hopes we hold for this sacrifice—that the bread and wine will become the Body and Blood of Christ, and that it will nourish us in our discipleship.

This part of the Mass used to be called the offertory, but it is more properly called the preparation of the gifts. The real offering will take place later, during the eucharistic prayer. The priest and people have been preparing themselves and the altar for the offering that follows. The gifts being prepared at this time include our very lives. As this part of the Mass concludes, you can see the offerings placed on the altar. You may also visualize yourself up there with them, ever ready to give yourself in service to Christ.[97]

The Eucharistic Prayer

Although the priest alone recites aloud almost all the words of the eucharistic prayer, the whole congregation joins with Christ in proclaiming God's mighty deeds and offering the sacrifice. It takes concentration to pray along with the priest, but it is essential for all to do so. He offers the prayer on behalf of the entire community. It is not his personal prayer. He needs full participation to contribute to its weight.[98]

The priest may incense the offerings, the cross, and the altar. Another minister incenses the priest and the people.

The prayer is called *eucharistic* because it is "an act of thanksgiving." It is also a prayer of consecration. We believe that at the words of the priest the Holy Spirit changes the bread and wine into the Body and Blood of Christ. However, that is but one moment in the entire prayer.

As the eucharistic prayer begins, all may call to mind the blessings for which they are grateful. These may include family, home, job, or Church. They may also include the coming of Jesus Christ as savior, friend, and Lord.

97. See GIRM, 73–77.
98. See STL, 176–183.

> The Eucharistic Prayer . . . is the high point of the whole celebration.
>
> —*General Instruction of the Roman Missal,* 30

Ten eucharistic prayers are provided for use in the Roman Catholic Church. As mentioned earlier in this book, the first, also called the Roman Canon, is quite ancient and ornate. The second is based on another ancient text, reworked for clarity of words and structure. The third eucharistic prayer was newly composed after the Second Vatican Council. The fourth is also new, but it is based on an ancient prayer.

Three additional eucharistic prayers were specially composed for Masses with children (published in their own volume apart from the Missal). Two more were written for Masses with a theme of reconciliation. Another eucharistic prayer was written for Masses for various needs and occasions, and it comes in four variations; these almost make them sound like four distinct eucharistic prayers instead of one.

Certain guidelines govern the choice of the eucharistic prayer.[99] Prayers I and III are especially suited for Sundays; Prayer II for weekdays. Either II or III is appropriate for a Mass for the Dead. Eucharistic Prayer IV has an unchangeable preface, so it is used on occasions such as Sundays in Ordinary Time. At any Mass the priest usually chooses the one he thinks best fits the particular celebration at hand.

Most of the eucharistic prayers follow the same structure. They begin with a dialogue between the priest and the people. The priest invites the people to lift their hearts and give thanks to God. This solemn, extended dialogue has opened the eucharistic prayer since at least the fourth century.

The priest then prays the preface, which introduces the reasons why we are giving thanks and praise to God today. On certain days of the year only one preface may be used. Other days present options. No preface asks God to do anything. Every preface expresses thanks and praise. It often captures the themes of the season, feast, or occasion for celebration.

The preface leads directly to the Sanctus. We all join with the angels in singing a hymn of praise to God. Some have argued that this is the most important song to sing at any Mass because it lifts our voices with the singing of angels and saints, with humanity and indeed all creation in praise of God. The Hebrew word *Hosanna* is related to the word for "Jesus" (*Yeshua*), and it praises God as the one who saves us.

99. See GIRM, 365 and RS, 51–56.

In the United States the people kneel after the Sanctus as the priest continues to express words of praise to God. These vary in length. In Eucharistic Prayer II, for example, the words are quite brief. But in Eucharistic Prayer IV they are rather lengthy.

A solemn shift occurs when the priest asks God to send the Holy Spirit upon the offerings so that they may become the Body and Blood of Christ. This petition is called the *epiclesis*, or "the calling-down prayer." An explicit prayer for the coming of the Holy Spirit appears in all the eucharistic prayers except the first. You will see the priest extend his hands over the bread and the wine for this critical moment in the Mass. If a deacon is assisting, he kneels.

> It is truly right and just, our duty and our
> duty and our salvation,
> always and everywhere to give
> you thanks,
> Lord, holy Father, almighty
> and eternal God,
> through Christ our Lord.
>
> —Preface I for Advent

The institution narrative is the best-known part of the eucharistic prayer. The priest repeats the words that Jesus spoke at the Last Supper when he instituted the Eucharist. In the Roman Rite, we believe that the consecration of the bread and wine takes place with the institution narrative. Although it may appear that the priest is addressing these words to the people ("Take this, all of you"), he is still talking to God the Father as he does throughout the rest of the eucharistic prayer. Here he quotes for the Father the words that Jesus spoke to his disciples. The priest is telling the Father that one of the most important reasons we give thanks and praise is what Jesus did for us at the Last Supper. These are not only words of consecration; they are words of thanksgiving.

Still, because they are words of consecration, the liturgy pauses for a moment of adoration. The priest shows the elements to the people. It may look as though he is raising them in offering to the Father, but he is showing the Body and Blood of Christ. Many worshippers look down in humility, but it would be more appropriate to gaze prayerfully at the host and chalice. That is why the priest is showing them to the people.

The ringing of bells at this time is optional. Prior to the liturgical reforms following the Second Vatican Council, a server rang bells at the consecration of every Mass, while the priest recited the words in a low voice, facing the church's back wall. The bells alerted the people that he was raising the host and the chalice for their adoration. Today the people can usually see the priest's actions and hear his words spoken aloud in their own language. The need for bells has diminished. Some parishes keep them; others do not.

In the acclamation that follows the consecration, all express their faith and hope in words addressed to Jesus Christ. The priest addresses the body of the eucharistic prayer to the Father, but the people make this acclamation to Jesus Christ. Recall that at the end of the Gospel all say, "Praise to you, Lord Jesus Christ" because Jesus is truly present in his spoken word. Now at the end of the institution narrative all address words to Jesus Christ again because he is truly present under the forms of bread and wine.

This acclamation is sometimes called the memorial acclamation partly because of the words of remembrance that the priest says afterwards. In the acclamation to Christ, the people proclaim his death and Resurrection, and the priest then expresses virtually the same idea to the Father. He says that the community is calling to mind the death and Resurrection of Christ and looking forward to his Second Coming.

> We proclaim your Death, O Lord,
> and profess your Resurrection
> until you come again.
>
> —Memorial Acclamation

In doing so, the priest offers to God this holy and living sacrifice. When we speak about the "sacrifice of the Mass," we are speaking about this particular moment. Throughout the preparation of the gifts, as the bread and wine were prepared and placed on the altar, worshippers symbolically placed their own personal gifts on the altar as well. In the words after the acclamation, the priest offers the sacrifice to God. We believe that at Mass we are present again to the sacrifice of Christ on Calvary. As God was unfailingly pleased with the sacrifice of his Son, so we pray that God will find our inferior sacrifice acceptable as well. We have done all we can to express our faith and devotion, to purify ourselves of wrongdoing, and to appear pleasing before God. In this moment the priest makes the actual offering to God. He explicitly says, "we offer you this sacrifice." It is a key moment in the entire Mass.

The priest mentions the Holy Spirit in the next section of almost every eucharistic prayer. Some people have called this a "secondary epiclesis." However, the priest is not so much calling down the Spirit again, as he is acknowledging that when we all receive Communion, we will become one body, one Spirit in Christ. He is praying for unity, of which the Spirit is the source.

The eucharistic prayer includes petitions for the living and the dead.

Other petitions conclude the eucharistic prayer. These may be for the Church and our leaders, as well as for the living and the dead. The petitions in the Roman Canon pray only for faithful members of the Catholic Church, but the other eucharistic prayers expand the range. They even pray for nonbelievers who seek God with a sincere heart. In most of the eucharistic prayers we express our concern for Christians and non-Christians alike.

The eucharistic prayer concludes with an acclamation of praise. The priest gives all glory and honor to the Father through, with and in Jesus Christ in the unity of the Holy Spirit. His words summarize much of what we believe about prayer in general. We principally offer prayer to the Father. The Holy Spirit helps us to pray as we ought. We offer prayer through Jesus Christ as our intercessor, with him because he also prays to the Father, and in him because we are members of his Body.

The priest elevates the vessels for this final acclamation. Holding in his hands the elements of our sacrifice, he lifts them high to God. They are the principal reasons for which this community give thanks, the reasons why this prayer is eucharistic.

To all of this the faithful answer "Amen." The word is short. But it adds the voice of the people to seal the entire prayer of thanksgiving. We give thanks and praise to God. We recall the mighty deeds that God has done. We witness the consecration of the bread and wine. We offer ourselves in sacrifice to God. We pray for the needs of the Church and the world. We do all of this throughout the entire eucharistic prayer, but especially when we say its final word. Amen. Amen to all that God has done and continues to do in our sight.[100]

The Communion Rite

The highlight of the Communion rite, and of the entire Mass, is eating and drinking the Body and Blood of Christ. This is the sacrament par excellence of the Church. All the parts of the Communion rite build up to the sharing of Communion.[101]

100. See GIRM, 78–79 and 216–236.

101. See GIRM, 80–89, 149–152, 237–249 and STL, 184–185.

The Lord's Prayer

The rite begins with the Lord's Prayer, deliberately juxtaposed with the eucharistic prayer. Once the eucharistic prayer is completed, we stand in the presence of the Body and Blood of Christ. What do we say? The best idea is to say the prayer that Jesus taught.

The priest's introduction to the Lord's Prayer includes the words "we dare to say." These are inspired by a third-century treatise on the Lord's Prayer by St. Cyprian. Many of the prayers of the Mass call God "Lord" or some other majestic term of greatness. To call God "Father" is bold because of its intimacy. Nonetheless, by our Baptism we are children of God by adoption. Jesus Christ is the incarnate child of God, born of the Father and of the Virgin Mary. But we are adopted children of God, born through Baptism. We are all entitled to call God our Father because Jesus taught us to use that word. He called God his Father, and he invites us to do the same. Hence, "we dare" to call God Father.

As adopted sons and daughters of God we are given the courage to call him Father.

The Lord's Prayer appears twice in the Bible—once in Matthew's account of the Gospel and once in Luke's. During the Mass we follow Matthew's version, which has a slightly richer content. Some scholars think that Luke's version is an earlier version because it is easier to explain why Matthew added some lines than to explain why Luke deleted them. In the end it doesn't matter. Both are part of the inspired Gospel accounts. Nearly all Christians use Matthew's version in their devotional prayer, so it rightly takes a central place in the celebration of the Mass.

All of us sing or say the Lord's Prayer together. It belongs to all the people of God. This is not a time for a solo, nor for a paraphrase of the prayer that Jesus taught.[102]

After the Lord's Prayer, however, the priest alone offers the embolism, an insertion into the prayer. Springing from the theme of the final petition, the embolism asks God to deliver us from all evil and to grant us peace. All

102. See STL, 186.

respond with a line that many associate with the way that non-Catholic Christians conclude the Lord's Prayer: "For the kingdom, the power and the glory are yours, now and for ever." Some early versions of the Gospel according to Matthew included that acclamation at the end of the Lord's Prayer, but it is missing from the earliest manuscripts of the Gospel. The Catholic Church retains the earliest Biblical tradition of the Lord's Prayer, but in a gesture of openness to the spiritual customs of other Christian Churches, the acclamation appears in the Catholic Mass after the embolism.[103]

Sign of Peace

Peace is one of the great themes of the Communion rite. The priest quotes Jesus' promise of peace and prays for the peace and unity of the Church. Then he introduces a dialogue in which he explicitly expresses the same theme: "The peace of the Lord be with you always." The deacon or the priest may then invite all to exchange a sign of peace. The deacon may make this invitation because he has some responsibility for keeping order throughout the service. For example, he may at times invite people to kneel or stand. He will give the dismissal at the end of the Mass. Here, in keeping with his job of managing actions, he invites people to exchange a sign of peace.

The peace is a sign of Christian communion. It foreshadows the communion that all will share in the Sacrament of the Eucharist. The sign of peace is not a time to say hello, to introduce yourself for the first time to those who are nearby, to make plans for activities after Mass, to catch up on the news, or to check messages on a cellular device. It is a time for exchanging—and building—peace. Remember that catechumens may have been dismissed earlier. Only baptized Christians authentically share this peace. This sign does not symbolize forgiveness or reconciliation; it signifies the peace that does exist—not one that ought to exist. Christians share membership in the Body of Christ. This membership, this mutual peace, they share with one another.

> The Church entreats peace and unity for herself and for the whole human family.
>
> —*General Instruction of the Roman Missal*, 82

A person need not share peace with absolutely everyone. Nor should the priest share peace up and down the aisle. The peace does not come from

103. See GIRM, 81 and 153.

the priest. It exists within the Body of Christ, and it is shared among the Body of Christ.[104]

Lamb of God and the Fraction of the Bread

The Lamb of God accompanies the fraction of the bread. As mentioned earlier in this resource, according to the Acts of the Apostles, the Sunday Eucharist was first known as the breaking of bread. This solemn moment in the liturgy expresses much of who we are as a Church. As Jesus was broken for us on the cross, as he poured out his Blood for us, so the bread is broken. Its pieces are to be shared, so that all may partake of one loaf as one body. In some parishes the priest uses a large host that can be broken into many pieces. Even when using a small host, he should share with others some of what he breaks. This best expresses the sacrifice and unity that we experience as the Body of Christ.

The sign of peace is a rite for the baptized, the members of the Body of Christ.

During this action, all sing the Lamb of God. This traditional litany cries out to Jesus Christ as the lamb slain in sacrifice for us. He is the lamb of the new covenant, slaughtered, yet standing as the Risen Christ. We ask for his mercy and peace as we witness the breaking of bread upon the altar. Additional tropes other than "Lamb of God" are no longer permitted.[105] In many churches people kneel after the Lamb of God to prepare to receive Communion. However, the local bishop may permit people to remain standing, drawing more unity into the different parts of the Communion rite.[106]

Invitation to Holy Communion

The priest says two prayers privately to prepare for his own Communion. Then he holds up a piece of the broken host and proclaims aloud that this is

104. See GIRM, 82, 154; RS, 71–72; and STL, 188.
105. See STL, 188.
106. See GIRM, 83, 155; NDRHC, 37–40; and RS, 73; STL, 188.

the Lamb of God who takes away the sins of the world. He is quoting John the Baptist, who pointed out Jesus to his own disciples with a similar expression. As John invited them to follow Jesus, so we follow the same Lamb of God—through sacrifice and glory.

The priest declares that we who are called to the supper of the Lamb are blessed. He is quoting a line from Revelation.[107] When we partake of this communion, we receive sustenance for our daily living. We also receive a foretaste of the heavenly banquet that awaits the faithful at the end of time.

The Communion song begins as the priest receives Communion.

Together with the priest we respond that we are not worthy to receive Christ in this Communion. We are echoing the statement of the centurion who asked Jesus to cure his daughter. The centurion said that he was not worthy for Jesus to enter under the roof of his home. He suggested that Jesus simply say a word of healing from afar, confident that this alone would bring the desired effect for his daughter. Jesus praised the man's faith, and the man's daughter was cured. The practice of reciting this line probably originated in the Middle Ages on occasions when the priest brought Communion to the sick. The sick prayed for healing and expressed their unworthiness to receive the awesome mystery of Holy Communion. Yet before we declare our unworthiness, the priest has proclaimed blessed those who share in the supper of the Lamb. Although we humans are not worthy to receive Christ and to be one with him, we are blessed because we may partake in this Communion.[108]

Receiving Communion

When people come to Communion, they leave their place, process to the station, and stand before the minister. There they are to slightly lower and raise their head, much as they may do when saying the name of Jesus. This small

107. See Revelation 19:6-9.

108. See GIRM, 157–158.

sign of respect shows their recognition of the awesome mystery of Christ's Body broken for us. The minister says, "The Body of Christ." Each one answers "Amen" with a firm voice. With this "Amen" the faithful affirm the Sacrament of the Body of Christ. It is their statement of faith in the one who suffered and died for all.

Worshippers may receive the Body of Christ either in the mouth or in the hand, according to their own preference. If they receive in the mouth, they open it and extend their tongue. This will help the minister place the host in the mouth without dropping it. A server holding a communion-plate can help catch a falling host. If people receive in the hand, communicants place their strong hand beneath their weak hand. For example, for those who are right handed, the minister places the host in the palm of their left hand. Communicants do not take the host from the minister with their fingers; they receive it like a beggar. They place the host in their mouth immediately and then proceed to the next station.[109]

> It is most desirable that the faithful, just as the Priest himself is bound to do, receive the Lord's Body from hosts consecrated at the same Mass.
>
> —*General Instruction of the Roman Missal,* 85

Some people make the sign of the cross after receiving Communion. It is a pious custom, though not required as is bowing one's head before receiving Communion. When you think about it, making the sign of the cross can add nothing more valuable than the Communion just received.

The faithful are encouraged to participate in Communion under both kinds.[110] "Holy Communion has a fuller form as a sign when it takes place under both kinds. For in this form the sign of the Eucharistic banquet is more clearly evident and clearer expression is given to the divine will by which the new and eternal Covenant is ratified in the Blood of the Lord, as also the connection between the Eucharistic banquet and the eschatological banquet in the Kingdom of the Father."[111]

If a minister is offering Communion from the chalice, communicants go to that station next. Once again, they bow their head in the sacramental presence of Christ. The minister will say, "The Blood of Christ." Each

109. See NDRHC, 41–50.
110. See GIRM, 281–287; NDHRC, 17–21, 23–30; and RS, 100–107.
111. GIRM, 281.

communicant answers, "Amen." They accept the cup into their own hands and take a sip. Then they hand the cup back to the minister, who will wipe the rim with a purificator and turn the vessel for the next communicant. All return to their places in turn.

Many Catholics kneel in their pew for a few moments of private prayer. Some sit. The bishop may also permit the whole congregation to stand throughout Communion time. Whatever posture people assume, they think about the great mystery in which they partake, and the unity they are forming with other communicants.

The faithful are encouraged to receive both species to share in the full sign of Christ's presence.

All join in the Communion song. The music is another way that the entire community expresses its unity in the Body and Blood of Christ. We are so uplifted by the experience that all we can do is sing.[112]

At Mass in many churches some people receive Communion from previously consecrated hosts that have been kept in the tabernacle. The Church's official liturgical books never recommend this practice, even though it is widespread. The ideal is for the faithful to receive Communion from the bread and wine consecrated at the Mass they attend. Earlier in the Mass the bread, wine, and contributions for the Church were carried to the altar in the procession of the gifts. These symbolize the offering that each one makes. During the eucharistic prayer, the Holy Spirit has changed the bread and wine into the Body and Blood of Christ, and the faithful have associated themselves with the offering of Christ on the cross. Now the fruits of the sacrifice are returned to the faithful. All the prayers, intentions, and praise that they offered at this Mass have been invested in the bread and wine. Now the same bread and wine comes to them consecrated as the Body and Blood of Christ. When people receive Communion from the tabernacle, they are receiving the Body of Christ, but they do not participate fully in the Mass currently being celebrated. The priest is required to receive

112. See STL, 189–195.

> The Communion Chant . . . [expresses] the spiritual union of the communicants by means of the unity of their voices, to show gladness of heart, and to bring out more clearly the "communitarian" character of the procession to receive Eucharist.
>
> —*General Instruction of the Roman Missal*, 86

Communion from the bread and wine consecrated at each Mass. Even concelebrants must do so. They may not receive Communion from the tabernacle because the nature of the Mass demands that they eat and drink the Body and Blood consecrated in the same sacrifice. As much as possible, the priest is supposed to offer each communicant the same level of participation.

After all have received Communion, the priest or deacon purifies the vessels. This process is called "purification" because he will swallow any leftover crumbs of the consecrated bread and droplets of the consecrated wine.[113] When the priest does this, he recites a quiet prayer from the fifth century. Although most people never hear it, it is one of the oldest and loveliest prayers of the Mass: "What has passed our lips as food, O Lord, may we possess in purity of heart, that what has been given to us in time may be our healing for eternity." After Mass someone else may wash the vessels with soap and water.

All may sit for a few moments of silent thanksgiving. To receive Communion is to have a personal encounter with the Risen Christ. A song after Communion does the same.[114] The Communion procession and the Communion song have focused on communal activity. Giving thanks in silence is also a communal gesture, but it allows each one to formulate thoughts of gratitude for a few moments.[115]

Prayer after Communion

All stand for the prayer after Communion. With rare exception, we stand for prayers at Mass. Whenever we address God directly, we do it standing up. This posture shows respect, and it symbolizes the Resurrection. On the last day, we hope to rise up with Christ to stand in the presence of God. Especially for this prayer after Communion, when we have just received the Sacrament of the Risen Christ, our posture demonstrates our belief in the Resurrection.[116]

113. See GIRM, 278–280 and NDRHC, 51–55.
114. STL, 196.
115. See GIRM, 84–88, 159–165 and RS, 80–96.
116. See GIRM, 89 and STL, 197.

Some people do not present themselves for Communion. Some of these are not members of the Catholic Church. Some are children younger than the age for first Communion. Some feel that they are in a state of grave sin. Some are living in a marriage not recognized by the Church. For whatever reason, some people do not receive Communion. Almost every time the priest offers the prayer after Communion, he assumes that everyone who joins him in that prayer has just joined him in Communion. People not receiving Communion benefit from the Mass in other ways, but they do not fully participate in what the Mass offers. Thankfully, the Catholic Church has ways to help many people begin or return to the practice of receiving the Body and Blood of Christ. Pastors can help wayward faithful return to the sacraments under the proper conditions through an annulment, a convalidation, the sacrament of reconciliation, and even a perfect act of contrition.[117]

The Concluding Rites

Before we leave the celebration, we resolve a few final matters. We make connections between the Eucharist we have celebrated and the ministry of the upcoming week. We receive a final blessing. And we hear our commission to bring Christ to the world.[118]

Announcements

The announcements spread news of activities that will take place during the upcoming week. These should provide ways to put one's faith into action. Your parish may offer educational sessions, social events, worship services, or apostolic activity. More information is usually available in the printed bulletin that people can take home or on the parish website. People should familiarize themselves with these events and look for ways to share their faith each week.

> Go and announce the Gospel of the Lord.
>
> —Dismissal

Announcements are to be made after the prayer after Communion. They should not interrupt the silence that follows the sharing of Communion and that the priest's prayer brings to a close.[119]

117. See *Catechism of the Catholic Church* (CCC), 1452.
118. See GIRM, 90, 166–170, 184–186, 250–251 and STL, 198–199.
119. See GIRM, 90A.

Final Blessing

When the announcements are over, the priest says, "The Lord be with you." These words are still called a greeting, even though he says them near the end of the service. He used a similar greeting near the beginning of Mass and to start the eucharistic prayer. A greeting also introduces the Gospel. Like a bell, these words signal that something important is about to follow. In this case, what follows is the blessing and dismissal.

Sometimes the blessing is elaborate. The deacon or priest may command the people to bow down for it. He's asking for more than a bow of the head. This time everyone bows from the waist to receive the blessing from on high. Sometimes the priest addresses God directly in words called a "prayer over the people." During Lent, the priest may give a prayer over the people at the end of Mass every day. He may offer one at other times of year as well. On other occasions the priest may give a solemn blessing, using words that he addresses to the people, rather than to God. The solemn blessing usually splits into three parts. The people answer "Amen" to each part. In truth, it's hard to tell when each part is ending, so sometimes the congregation's response is weak. But people will get the idea if they know what to expect and pay attention to the words the priest is saying.[120]

The expanded blessing may fit the circumstances of a particular occasion. Baptisms and weddings, for example, conclude with their own solemn blessings. Or the priest may offer a prayer from the *Book of Blessings* on some individual, such as a departing parishioner.

The deacon or the priest issues the dismissal. This may take different forms, some of them encouraging the people to live the Gospel throughout the coming week. As they have participated fully in the liturgy, so they will participate fully in mission. The response is always the same, "Thanks be to God." This attitude of thanksgiving concludes the formal words of the Mass.[121]

Many parishes add a concluding song.[122] The Missal never refers to a concluding song, but singing has served well to provide closure to those who have gathered. As they began Mass with a song, so they conclude it. Nonetheless, one may confidently go forth from the church to instrumental music or even in silence. After all, the deacon has just invited the faithful to "Go." There is no need to sing another song. They are being sent into the

120. See GIRM, 90B.

121. See GIRM, 90C.

122. See STL, 199.

world to share the Good News of Christ, to serve the needs of others, and to invite those they meet to share the Church's life. Now is the time to start.

The Concluding Rites send us forth on Christ's mission in the world.

Many Catholics sign themselves with holy water on the way out, but the liturgical books never mention it. Using holy water on the way into church as a reminder of Baptism helps people prepare for Mass, but after receiving Communion they have all the equipment they need for the mission that lies beyond the door.

The very word *mass* comes from this part of the service. In Latin, the deacon says, Ite, missa est. The word missa is related to the English words mission and dismissal. It sends people forth with a purpose. The very title of the service for which we gather each week tells us that we will be sent forth. We will return next Sunday with the fruits of our ministry to worship God once again.

Preparation Basics

If preparing a Mass feels like a formidable task, here are some of the basics to get you started.

- **The day**. Know what liturgical day is being observed on the calendar. You may learn this quickly from an ordo or by checking the website of the United States Conference of Catholic Bishops. The complete liturgical calendar for the current year can be accessed at www.usccb.org/about/divine-worship/liturgical-calendar/index.cfm.[123]
- **The occasion**. At times a liturgy is prepared because of a particular occasion, such as a confirmation, a wedding, or a funeral. Those occasions may be subject to the day in the liturgical calendar. For example, a

123. See also GIRM, 353–355.

wedding Mass that is being prepared on the same day as the parish's patronal solemnity will use the prayers and readings of the solemnity. Consult the annual calendar on the USCCB website for guidance.

- **The Lectionary.** The readings for the Mass are found in the Lectionary. Become familiar with this book so that you can find the appropriate readings for the celebration at hand. The USCCB publishes the daily readings in English and in Spanish. Near the top of the page you will see a Lectionary number that coincides with the number on the matching section of the printed volume. Note that these are Lectionary numbers, not page numbers. They function like hundreds of chapter headings throughout the Lectionary.[124]
- **The Missal.** Your priest will probably know where to find the appropriate prayers in the Missal, but you can help by becoming familiar with its many parts. The two most commonly-used sections are the Proper of Time and the Proper of Saints. Once you know the liturgical day being observed, you can find the appropriate prayers for the day in the proper section of the Missal.[125]
- **Music**. If possible, arrange for singing the entrance song, the Gospel acclamation, the Sanctus, the memorial acclamation, the Amen, and the Communion song. Those are the most basic parts for music. Singing them will invite congregational participation at the appropriate times, while highlighting the significant parts of the Mass.[126]
- **Participation**. Prepare for all the people to participate in this liturgy. Solicit ministers from among the faithful. Provide suitable participation aids with the necessary songs and responses. Welcome all when they arrive. Give them places where they can clearly see and hear what is happening. Teach the music that they may not know. Encourage their full attention. School all ministers in communicating effectively with all who have come. The liturgy is not executed by one or two ministers. It demands the full, conscious, active participation of all.[127]

124. See also GIRM, 357–362.

125. See also GIRM, 363–365 and RS, 58–59.

126. See also GIRM, 366–367. Those who prepare the Sunday Mass should review the guidelines found in *Sing to the Lord: Music in Divine Worship*.

127. It will be helpful for those who prepare Sunday Mass to also refer to GIRM, 117–119 regarding specific things that need to be prepared such as the altar, candles, Lectionary, and so on.

Integrating Other Rituals into the Mass

At times the Mass will include some other ceremony. If the ceremony comes from another official liturgical book, you will find guidance in the introductory material of that book. Here are some common celebrations you may encounter, along with some advice on what to expect.[128]

Baptism of Children

The Baptism of children commonly takes place apart from Mass. Many parishes establish a time on Sundays after the morning Masses for this ceremony, and a deacon or priest may preside. However, the ceremony may be incorporated into a regularly scheduled Sunday Mass.[129]

The liturgy begins at the door of the church, where the procession usually forms. However, before starting the procession, the community may sing a short entrance song—perhaps one verse of the scheduled opening hymn. This will account for the entrance antiphon in the Missal and will gather the voices of the community.

A Baptism at Sunday Mass will evangelize the parish about the rites of the Church and the communal dimension of Baptism.

128. Refer to RS, 75–79 on the joining of various rites with the celebration of Mass.

129. See the Rite of Baptism for Children (RBC), 29 for details.

Then from the door of the church the priest makes the sign of the cross. Omitting the greeting and the penitential act, he receives the children using the formulas from the Rite of Baptism,[130] and then processes with the ministers to the sanctuary. The Liturgy of the Word follows. The creed is omitted. The universal prayer takes place, and the short litany of the saints is added.[131] Then the Baptism takes place according to its own ceremonies.[132] Afterwards, the Mass continues in the usual way with the procession of the gifts.

At the end of Mass, the priest may use one of the blessing formulas from the Rite of Baptism.[133]

First Communion

Surprisingly, there are no special ceremonies in any liturgical book that pertain to the celebration of first Communion, even though it is a major event in parishes every year. Many communities have added activities to the liturgy, but none of these is required, and they can actually detract from the celebration at hand. At its simplest, the children may simply present themselves in the Communion line at the appropriate time.

In the opening procession, first communicants may enter behind the cross and candles, and before the minister carrying the *Book of the Gospels*. If a sufficient number of children are present, the liturgy may include adaptations allowed in the Vatican's *Directory for Masses with Children*—abbreviating prayers and readings, enhancing the Gospel procession, and using a eucharistic prayer for Masses with children, for example.

Children may help provide decoration or music for the celebration, but none of this is required. The celebration will probably include the readings and prayers of the liturgical day. However, the Lectionary's fourth volume includes recommendations for a first Communion Mass among its ritual Masses. These may be used when no solemnity intervenes—for example, if the first Communion Mass takes place on a weekday in Ordinary Time.

Anointing of the Sick

A priest may anoint the sick within Mass. The official book for this ritual is *Pastoral Care of the Sick: Rites of Anointing and Viaticum*. The explanation

130. See RBC, 33–43.
131. See RBC, 47–48.
132. See RBC, 49–66.
133. See RBC, 70, 247–249.

for celebrating this sacrament within Mass begins at 131.

After the sign of the cross and the greeting, the priest welcomes the sick. He offers an appropriate collect. The Liturgy of the Word takes place as usual. If the day is not a Sunday or other day of high rank, special readings may be used.

The liturgy of anointing follows the homily. It begins with a litany, then continues with the laying on of hands and the prayer over the oil. Then the priest anoints the forehead and hands of the sick, who answer "Amen" to each part of the formula. The priest offers a prayer after the anointing, and the rest of the Mass continues as usual. He may use special prayers from the ritual book or the Missal for this occasion.

The liturgy of anointing follows the homily.

It would aid the priest if someone could keep a record of the individuals who present themselves for the anointing. That will enable the parish to maintain good records and follow up with other pastoral care.

Matrimony

A wedding may take place during the course of a regularly scheduled Sunday Mass.[134] In that case, the prayers and readings for that Sunday are used, not the ritual Mass for weddings in the Missal and Lectionary. However, on a Sunday in Ordinary Time, one of the readings may be taken from the Lectionary's collection of Masses for weddings.

The couple may enter the church in procession, as they would at a specially scheduled wedding. The presider conducts the ceremony after the homily. The creed comes after the universal prayer, not before,[135] in order to keep the petitions connected to the wedding ceremony.

134. See *Order of Celebrating Matrimony* (OCM), 34.
135. See OCM, 69.

The inclusion of a wedding at Sunday Mass is an evangelizing opportunity to catechize the faithful about the Catholic wedding ritual.

Weddings at the Sunday Mass allow the entire community to witness and celebrate the couple's matrimony. They may also help people learn how a Catholic wedding is to take place and which music and ceremonies are most important.

Blessings

The *Book of Blessings* includes a number of occasions when a blessing may take place during the course of Mass. Some do not take place at Mass for obvious reasons—the blessing of a new home or the blessing of animals, for example. For the rest, including the blessing of new extraordinary ministers of Holy Communion, the blessing takes place with the universal prayer. Other blessings, such as the one on Mothers' Day, are joined to the final blessing.

Wedding Anniversary

Many couples celebrating a twenty-fifth, fortieth, or fiftieth wedding anniversary ask for a blessing at church. The Order of Celebrating Matrimony includes prayers for this occasion in its third appendix. It presumes that the celebration is taking place within Mass.

The readings and prayers for the Mass are subject to the liturgical calendar. Because this is not a sacrament, but the anniversary of a sacrament, it is likely that the prayers and readings of the day take precedence. However, if the celebration is a weekday without some other solemnity or feast that must be observed, the liturgical texts may be drawn from those in the appropriate sections of the Missal and Lectionary for the anniversary of Marriage.

After the homily, the priest invites the couple to renew their commitment by praying silently.[136] Or, they may recite formulas that thank God for the gift of their Marriage.[137] Note that the couple do not repeat the words they said on their wedding day. Those words constitute the sacramental formula of marriage, and they are said only once: on the wedding day. The priest may then bless new rings or incense the original ones.[138]

The Mass resumes, and after the Lord's Prayer the priest may offer a special prayer of blessing for the couple. This imitates the style and occasion of the nuptial blessing from the wedding Mass. Another blessing concludes the service.

The basic structure of the Mass is unchanged, but these extra elements add to the spirit of joy that the community shares in the long commitment of the couple.

Liturgical Roles

In additional to the priest and deacon, other ministers play a role in the celebration of the Mass. The GIRM outlines these roles and how the minsters are to be involved in the Mass.[139]

The acolyte assists the priest at the altar by holding and arranging books and vessels. The GIRM uses the word *acolyte*[140] for a male who has been instituted into this ministry in a special ceremony over which a bishop presides. In practice, most acolytes are seminarians in preparation for priesthood and candidates preparing for the diaconate. These may also administer Holy Communion to the faithful whenever the number of priests and deacons is insufficient.

136. See OCM, 240–241.
137. See OCM, 242.
138. See OCM, 243–244.
139. See GIRM, 98–107.
140. See GIRM, 98–100.

More commonly, the role of the acolyte is divided between extraordinary ministers of Holy Communion and altar servers. After the priest has received Communion, the Communion ministers approach the altar, receive Communion, receive their Communion vessels, and administer Communion to other members of the faithful at designated stations. Altar servers fulfill a variety of responsibilities such as carrying the processional cross and candles, holding the Missal for the presider, arranging vessels on the altar, carrying water to the deacon or the priest, and washing the priest's hands. They may also assist by carrying incense and ringing bells.

A lector proclaims the readings that precede the Gospel. The GIRM restricts the word *lector* to those males whom a bishop institutes into this ministry.[141] Lectors properly called are usually seminarians in preparation for the priesthood and candidates in preparation for the diaconate.

However, other lay men and women may serve as readers. These will proclaim the first reading. If there is no psalmist, they lead the responsorial psalm. If there is a second reading, they proclaim it. If there is no deacon, the priest reads the Gospel, and a lay minister reads the petitions of the universal prayer.

Musicians lead the singing. Instrumentalists may accompany. A cantor (or leader of song) will help lead the congregational song. A choir may do the same or sing appropriate choral music. A psalmist may lead the responsorial psalm.

A sacristan will prepare books and vestments for the Mass. Many sacristans work with those preparing the liturgical environment to create a harmonious appearance for Catholic worship.

A commentator may give explanations at appropriate moments. Some of the explanations described in GIRM 31 may be assigned to the person holding this role. If the community has a gifted catechist, for example, that person could speak at such moments either before or during Sunday Mass.

> The celebration of the Eucharist . . . pertains to the whole Body of the Church, manifests it, and has its effect upon it. Indeed, it also affects the individual members of the Church in a different way, according to their different orders, functions, and actual participation.
>
> —*General Instruction of the Roman Missal*, 91

Ushers take up the collection, a service that reminds the faithful of

141. See GIRM, 99.

There are many ways for the liturgy to reflect cultural variety: music, gesture, environment, and language.

their fiscal responsibility, and of the sacrifice they make whenever they participate at Mass. Traditionally, laymen have fulfilled this role, but women may and do serve as ushers.

Greeters appear at the doors of the church to welcome those who are arriving, help them find their places, and answer questions about the building and the services that the parish offers.

Multicultural Concerns

Local communities are increasingly diverse, and the results can be seen in almost any Sunday assembly. Some parishes are more varied than others, but the growth of multiculturalism has brought opportunities and stresses to many people in the community.

At the most dramatic, the same parish may be offering independent Sunday Masses in different languages—gathering people of different ethnicities in separate celebrations.

The United States Conference of Catholic Bishops has published Guidelines for a Multicultural Celebration of Mass: www.usccb.org/prayer-and-worship/the-mass/frequently-asked-questions/guidelines-for-a-multilingual-celebration-of-mass.cfm. These recommend a variety of music, gesture, and environmental styles, as well as moderate use of commentary at appropriate moments in pertinent languages. One of the readings may be proclaimed in a minority language. The Gospel may be proclaimed twice, once in each language, but with only one concluding dialogue.

The homily should be in the dominant language, but a summary may be given in another one. The petitions may be offered in diverse languages, but the eucharistic prayer should be offered in only one language to preserve its unity. The people's acclamations may reflect different linguistic groups. All may recite the Lord's Prayer in their own language simultaneously, an action that forms its own unifying power in the recitation. Diverse languages may be used in the solemn blessing.

The music also may reflect the diversity of the group. Choirs of different ethnicities, for example, may contribute their gifts to various parts of the Mass.

Much of this demands an open heart by the people who are assembled, and they may gain much by experiencing worship with a variety of cultures beyond their own.

Intergenerational Concerns

Some of the diversity in any assembly is in its generational composition. Stereotypically, people of older generations give a higher priority to Mass participation than the younger generations, but younger people do also come. Some members of the older generation come to church because their lives are more flexible. They can more easily arrange time for a spiritual exercise that means much to them. They also bring a lifetime of experience in liturgical prayer upon which they may build. The nature of the Mass is that its meaning expands the more years one commits to participation.

Those who prepare the liturgy well try to appeal to as many groups as possible so that everyone can find a home.

Younger adults bring children, and many of them take pains to make this happen. They have made the Mass a priority, and they don't want to miss out on its fruits. They enjoy forming a community with others. They rejoice in the gift of the Eucharist. They bond as a family.

However, because of the generational mix, expectations differ. Younger Catholics find the repetitious nature of the Mass boring, whereas older Catholics find it inspiring. A homiletic style that appeals to young parents may leave older Catholics feeling left out. Crying babies may offend some members, while bringing delight to others. Music that has long inspired one generation strikes another generation as odd. Hospitality may seem genuine to some people but overbearing to others.

A single celebration of the Mass cannot appeal to everyone who comes. We are all human. We have our stylistic preferences. Those who prepare the liturgy well try to appeal to as many groups as possible so that everyone can find a home. Some variety in the styles of worship will demonstrate a genuine desire to listen to the needs of the people and to respond in ways that will help them praise God. Most importantly, worshippers will realize that a message that misses them this weekend may hit someone else very powerfully. The result can help build the entire community, even if it does not inspire absolutely everyone.

Individual worshippers can usually experience better spiritual growth if they commit to the same community from week to week. People who come to one experience of worship at your parish one time will find plenty to dislike. But once they make connections with others, once they invest in relationship, they will find much to enjoy. Good liturgical preparation also concerns good community development. Find ways to help the members of your community meet one another. They will grow in grace and friendship, and their experience of the Mass will flower.

Legitimate Adaptation

The rubrics for Mass include a number of places where options are allowed—such as the choice of music and of the presidential prayers.[142] Other parts of the Mass are not so flexible—such as the uses of the altar and the words of a eucharistic prayer. The final section of the GIRM addresses adaptations that belong to the conference of bishops.[143] The priest has some freedoms, too. "Where it is laid down by the rubrics, the celebrant is permitted to adapt

142. See GIRM, 31.
143. See GIRM, 386–399.

somewhat [certain explanations that are foreseen in the rite itself] so that they correspond to the capacity for understanding of those participating"[144] Liturgical adaptations are usually reserved to conferences of bishops and the Holy See.[145]

Sunday Mass as Catechesis and Formation

The Mass is a primary source of catechesis and formation. Many of its elements deserve intense study and reflection upon its meaning. Some people have been tempted to organize a catechetical Mass, in which the presider interrupts the celebration at critical moments to comment on the proceedings. However, this disrupts the purpose of the Mass, which is liturgical, rather than catechetical. The eucharistic prayer should never be interrupted for commentary.

The celebration of the Mass informs what we believe and how we live.

Nonetheless, the GIRM envisions several moments within the Mass when the presider or someone else may give commentary.[146] He may use his own words to introduce the Mass of the day after the greeting and before the Penitential Act. He may introduce the readings after the collect and before the first reading. He may express reasons for giving thanks after the prayer over the offerings and before the dialogue that opens the eucharistic prayer. He may offer concluding comments before the dismissal. In all these moments, he is to be sparing in his use of words.

The texts and actions of the Mass are aimed at worship, but they also instruct. The words at Mass shape what we believe. An old maxim—*Lex orandi, lex credendi*—expresses how the structure of prayer forms the structure of belief. Our faith is rooted in how we pray, and the forms of praying school us in our faith. These have a further impact in what some people call the *lex vivendi*. Prayer and belief in turn form the structure of how we live.

144. GIRM, 31.

145. See alsothe Fourth Instruction for the Right Application of the Conciliar Constitution on the Liturgy: *Inculturation and the Roman Liturgy*.

146. See GIRM, 31.

The more deeply people participate in the Mass, the richer their faith will grow, and the greater impact it will have on their lives.

Outside Mass, there are many opportunities for catechesis. Many worshippers have found the value of reflecting on the Scripture readings that they will hear on the following Sunday. A similar spiritual experience can be obtained by meditating on some of the other prayers at Mass. The collects, for example, usually pack a lot of thought into just a few words. Taking time with one will help uncover its complexity. The same may be said of the preface or the entire body of the eucharistic prayer. Catholics hear these words at every Mass, but they come and go so quickly that they rarely take time to ponder their meaning.

People would also benefit from thinking about the sacrifices that they are offering to God, as well as their reasons for giving thanks. Forming people to be conscious of these activities can enhance their experience at Mass.

Faithful members of the community may also learn through bulletin inserts or carefully recommended websites. Gatherings of parishioners or associations of the faithful provide additional opportunity for instruction and reflection.

Sunday Mass as Evangelization

Without question the Mass has a certain evangelical component. Some people make a rare visit to church when they come for a specific purpose—the Baptism of a child, a wedding anniversary, a funeral, Mothers' Day, Christmas or Easter. For people who hear the readings and prayers of the Mass infrequently, these are experiences in which the Gospel is proclaimed, applied, and explained for them.

> The Church evangelizes and is herself evangelized through the beauty of the liturgy, which is both a celebration of the task of evangelization and the source of her renewed self-giving.
>
> —*Evangelii gaudium*, 24

The dismissal that concludes the Mass is highly evangelical in its intent. It sends the faithful forth into the world to proclaim the Gospel of Christ. They are not simply leaving because Mass is over; they are commissioned to leave the building as a body with a mission. Those who dismiss themselves after receiving Communion without a good reason to do so demonstrate a poor appreciation of this point.

They should not leave the building when they got the Communion they came for; they should depart when they have received their commission to go forth.

On any day, having greeters available at your church will make it easier for visitors to feel welcome. If the atmosphere is friendly and engaging, if you give people a reason to return, your parish will evangelize.

Sunday Mass and Mission

One of the beautiful connections between Sunday Mass and the rest of life is the way that we consider our sacrificial offering. Many people think of their offering as the contribution they toss in the collection basket. It is, but we also offer much more.

> The Church which "goes forth" is a community of missionary disciples.
>
> —*Evangelii gaudium*, 24

In your preparations for Mass, you are sacrificing your time and talent for the sake of the Body of Christ. In your personal life, you sacrifice for the people you love and who depend on you for help.

You sacrifice for strangers you encounter in your daily work, drivers who pass you on the road. In all these actions you think less of yourself and more of someone else. You hope that these sacrifices are pleasing to God. They are a part of you, and you place them upon the altar at every Mass.

Perhaps the homily, a song, a prayer, or the Scriptures have touched you this week. Sometimes a passage you've heard many times suddenly reveals another layer of meaning because of the circumstances of your life. In these ways, you strengthen the connections between liturgy and life.

Concluding Remarks

You may have noticed that throughout this book, the commentary has spoken about "preparing the liturgy" rather than "planning the liturgy." The reason is simple. A short look at any liturgical book will reveal that the Church has already "planned" the liturgy. Your role is to prepare it.

The Church arranges the liturgical calendar, prepares books such as the Missal and Lectionary, communicates rubrics, and translates prayers. Your job is to take what has been planned for the universal Church and to prepare it for the place where you worship. To do so is to step inside the Catholic Church's vision and to apply it to a specific local good. You will draw from the well of the Church's wisdom, and you will share with others the fruit of your experience.

When we worship together in spite of our differences, we give fitting praise to God.

Preparing for Mass involves many people with different abilities and interests. From time to time, there are bound to be disagreements. The Missal foresees this in part of its opening remarks, and it offers good pastoral guidance: "There should be harmony and diligence among all those involved in the effective preparation of each liturgical celebration in accordance with the Missal and other liturgical books, both as regards the rites and as regards the pastoral and musical aspects."[147]

Catholics care about the Mass, as well we should. We feel strongly about it because it expresses the core of our belief. At the same time, the very nature of the Mass is to draw us closer in Communion. When we worship together in spite of our differences, we give fitting praise to God.

Those who prepare the liturgy humbly, in a spirit of collaboration, with charity toward those who have different preferences, will all be deeply formed by its mystery. Preparing for Mass is a great privilege, second only to celebrating it well.

147. GIRM, 111.

Frequently Asked Questions

1. What is the proper way to reverence the altar during the entrance procession, during the Mass (for example, crossing in front of the altar; gesture for readers/cantors), and during the closing procession? Does it make a difference if the tabernacle is in the sanctuary?

Proper reverences demonstrate the importance of two physical objects, the altar and the tabernacle, as well as the period of time when a Mass is taking place.

Here are three simple rules to remember:

- Genuflect to a tabernacle.
- Bow to an altar.
- After Mass has begun, do not genuflect to the tabernacle.

No reverence is ever made to the ambo. No reverence is made to the cross, except on Good Friday when the tabernacle is empty, and the genuflection is made instead to the cross.

Before Mass and upon entering the church, each person is to genuflect in the direction of the tabernacle. If the tabernacle is not located in the sanctuary, the faithful may appropriately visit that area upon entering the church, or at least genuflect in that direction.

During the entrance and concluding processions, as the ministers arrive at the edge of the sanctuary, they genuflect only if the tabernacle is located in the sanctuary. Otherwise, they omit the genuflection. They bow to the altar, except for the minister holding the Book of the Gospels, who makes no reverence because of the dignity of the book being carried.[148]

The GIRM does not give instructions for others who enter or leave the sanctuary, or who cross in front of the altar. However, the *Ceremonial of Bishops* asks them to make a profound bow to the altar.[149] Once Mass has

148. See GIRM, 274.
149. See GIRM, 72.

If the tabernacle is not in the sanctuary, the ministers are to bow to the altar.

begun, no reverences are made to the tabernacle. An exception may be the minister who puts a ciborium in the tabernacle after Communion. It is appropriate for that minister to genuflect to the ciborium before shutting the tabernacle door, as the priest or deacon does near the end of the liturgy on Holy Thursday.

The reason that genuflections to the tabernacle are inappropriate during the course of the Mass is that the liturgy focuses on what is taking place on the altar. Reverences change, therefore, depending on the times when Mass is underway.

2. What are the options for the placement of the tabernacle in the church?

A tabernacle is to be located in a noble place suitable for prayer.[150] It may be in the sanctuary or in a chapel connected to the church, but not on top of the altar.[151] It should also be accessible to those who use wheelchairs.[152]

Churches are built for the celebration of Mass, so the altar should be the place where the eyes of the faithful naturally turn.[153]

150. See GIRM, 314.
151. See GIRM, 315.
152. See BLS, 74.
153. See GIRM, 299.

3. Is it appropriate to combine the Gloria with the sprinkling rite?

No. The purpose of the Gloria differs from that of the sprinkling rite. Suggestions for music for the sprinkling can be found in appendix II of the Missal. After that music, the priest offers a short prayer, concluding the rite. If the same Mass calls for singing or saying the Gloria, it follows that prayer in a separate liturgical unit.

Sprinkling the assembly with blessed water is a separate rite and should never be combined with the Gloria.

4. Why should the Gloria be sung instead of recited? Is it ever appropriate to omit at Sunday Mass (outside of Advent and Lent)?

The Gloria is the text of a hymn. It is as dissatisfying to recite it as it would be to recite the words of "Were You There?"

The Gloria is omitted on the Sundays of Advent and Lent, and on November 2, All Souls' Day, even when it falls on a Sunday. Otherwise, it is not to be omitted from the Sunday liturgy. The Gloria is also sung during sacramental rites taking place within Mass, such as weddings, Baptisms, and Confirmation.

5. When are appropriate times throughout the year to replace the penitential act with the sprinkling rite?

The penitential act may be replaced with the sprinkling rite on any Sunday. The Missal says that it is especially appropriate to sprinkle during the Sunday Masses of Easter Time.[154]

154. See GIRM, 51.

Practically, whenever the parish holy water font is running low, it is appropriate to schedule sprinkling so that the water may be blessed during a Sunday Mass in the presence of the people.

6. Who writes the Prayer of the Faithful?

Several options are possible; one or two people from the liturgy committee, the deacon, or the pastor or liturgy director may prepare the Prayer of the Faithful. Remember, the intercessions are general in nature, not just specific (before the revised GIRM, they were referred to as just that—the General Intercessions). For example: *For Mary Smith and all who are suffering from illness, we pray*, versus, *For Mary Smith who is sick, we pray.*

Samples of intercession are found in Appendix V of *The Roman Missal*. All of these are meant to serve as models for the intercessions that are used in the parish each week.

A good rule of thumb for those who prepare the intercessions is to have the scripture of the day in one hand and any local newspaper in the other.

In general, the Prayer of the Faithful is offered first for the Church, then for public authorities and the salvation of the world, for those oppressed or burdened by various needs, and for the local community.[155]

7. In the case of local, national, and international tragedies (hate crimes, mass shootings, racist issues, or extreme weathers—tsunami, floods, fires, etc.), how might concern for these acts be appropriately integrated into the Mass? And should this be done?

The universal prayer is the best opportunity for raising local, contemporary concerns to God. The petitions may and ideally should be composed by the local community. When tragedies strike, people naturally want to pray for them. This is the very purpose of the universal prayer.

There are other possibilities. The cantor could mention the concern before announcing the opening hymn. The presider could incorporate it into his introduction to the Mass following the greeting.[156] The homilist may skillfully treat the issues in the light of the Word of God. Announcements could include notice of special prayers or activities that relate to the tragedy.

155. GIRM, 69.
156. See GIRM, 31.

The music selected for Catholic worship should always adhere to the liturgical norms.

In an extreme case during Ordinary Time, the bishop of the diocese could ask all parishes to use one of the Masses for Various Needs and Occasions, which would cause the presidential prayers including the Sunday collect to be replaced—but that cannot be done without his approval.[157]

8. What are ways that the Sunday Mass is connected to the greater life of the parish, the home, and one's mission in the world?

The Mass is the source and summit of the Church's life and ministry.[158] To it we bring the sacrifices and hopes of the past week, from it we receive inspiration to proclaim the Gospel to all those we meet. Sunday Mass is the most important of all the parish's activities. All these lead to and derive from the celebration.

At home, Catholics prepare for Mass through their daily experience of prayer, sacrifice, and communion. These activities reach their perfection when the family returns to church for the next Sunday Mass.

157. See GIRM, 374.

158. See CSL, 10 and *Lumen gentium*, 11.

The conclusion of the Mass sends the assembly out with a mission—to announce the Gospel and to glorify the Lord. The final command is "Go." We take the message of the Mass to all we meet.

9. Can projection screens be used to display art and music?

The universal Church has no guidelines pertaining to projection screens, though some conferences of bishops have taken up the subject. Projection screens are more popular in some parts of the world than in others.

When the GIRM speaks of sacred images, it cautions that they be arranged "so as not to draw the attention of the faithful to themselves and away from the celebration itself."[159] The same advice could be applied to images on screens.

Parishes should be aware that some images are copyrighted, and justice demands that a parish pay for and acknowledge their use.

10. Is praise and worship music appropriate for Catholic worship?

The Communion song should begin as the priest receives Communion, thus unifying the entire assembly under one song.

Praise and worship music can draw the community together and enliven the faithful, but all music falls within liturgical guidelines. Religious songs may precede the celebration of Mass. Songs within the celebration should honor their liturgical function—whether at the entrance, Communion, or at other times. The people of God are called to full, conscious, active participation, especially in the music.[160] They should not become bystanders to the liturgical music program.[161]

---

159. GIRM, 318.

160. See CSL, 14.

161. Refer to STL, 126–136 concerning the three judgments, one evaluation, for selecting liturgical music.

11. Why is it best to proclaim the responsorial psalm at the ambo?

The responsorial psalm is part of the Lectionary. It is a pure quotation from the Bible. Part of the Liturgy of the Word, it is best proclaimed or sung from the ambo.

The refrain is frequently a slight variation on a biblical text, but the verses are drawn from the Book of Psalms or from a canticle lifted from a different book of the Bible, making them an expression of the Word of God. Leading the psalm from the ambo gives it the dignity it deserves.

12. When should the Communion song begin at Mass?

The Communion song begins as the priest receives Communion.[162] This unites all receiving Communion under one song.

This probably works best if more than one musician leads the singing—one starting the song as the priest receives Communion, the other entering the line at the same time. Then the musicians switch positions.

13. How might a parish transition from retrieving hosts from the tabernacle during Mass to consecrating enough for a single Mass? Why is this important?

The easiest way to begin the transition is at daily Mass, where the number of communicants can more readily be judged. Try appointing a sacristan to adjust the number of hosts in the ciborium before the gifts are brought to the altar—whether up the aisle or from the credence table. The same principle can be applied to Sundays. Sacristans can gain the skill of judging the number of communicants even in a large assembly.

In smaller communities, the priest could use large hosts that serve twenty-four each for the entire congregation. The sacristan could set out two, three, or four of these, depending on the number of communicants. The priest can break the host in the appropriate number of portions.

Making the transition is important because the people participate more fully in the Mass when they are receiving Communion from the bread and wine consecrated therein. The priest is bound to receive Communion from the bread he consecrates, and it is most desirable that the faithful do the

162. See GIRM 86 and 159.

same.[163] This lends integrity to the sacrifice offered by the people of God, and to the communion they share in turn.

14. If the parish community has a large number of parishioners from another ethnic group, what is the best way to respond to their needs?

The USCCB publishes guidelines for multicultural liturgies on its website www.usccb.org/prayer-and-worship/the-mass/frequently-asked-questions/guidelines-for-a-multilingual-celebration-of-mass.cfm.

Separate Masses are often more gratifying to members of different ethnic and linguistic groups. However, a joint celebration can enrich everyone.

When more than one language is used at Mass, these may be represented in the music, the readings, the universal prayer, and the announcements. The homily may be delivered in the dominant language, and a summary given in another. The eucharistic prayer is to be prayed in one language.

At a minimum, a few announcements in a different language at the end of the service may suffice to reassure those who speak it of their inclusion in the heart of the community at worship.

15. Is it appropriate for members of the faithful to hold hands during the Our Father? Or to extend their hands in the orans position?

There are no official directives pertaining to the position of the hands of the faithful during the Our Father. In 1975, the Vatican's journal *Notitiae* observed that people were joining hands during the Our Father as a sign of communion, that the gesture was introduced spontaneously on personal initiative, and that it is not in the rubrics. But the Vatican neither encouraged nor forbade the practice.

In 1997, the Vatican's instruction, *On Certain Questions Regarding the Collaboration of the Non-Ordained Faithful in the Sacred Ministry of Priest*, said that deacons and laity should not use gestures proper to the priest. Some have argued that the laity may therefore not raise hands during the Our Father, but the context concerns the parts of the liturgy reserved to the priest, such as the body of the eucharistic prayer. The Our Father, of course, is shared.

---

163. See GIRM, 86.

Perhaps it is best to follow the lead of the 1975 instruction, which noted that the practice exists, but did not promote or forbid it.

16. How can our parish help members of the assembly participate better at Mass and to recognize that the Sunday Mass is the most important thing they do each week?

Your parish can encourage participation by complimenting parishioners when they do it well. You can also work harder at building the parish community by helping people to become better acquainted. When individual worshippers feel welcomed into the community and comfortable with one another, they relax, sing better, and enjoy their time at the liturgy. They offer more fitting praise to God through their mutual concern for one another.

The preparation of a good worship aid is one way to help worshippers feel welcome and confident with the music they are to sing at Mass.

The parish leadership should also take a hard look at the budget for music. Offering better salaries can attract better musicians. When the music improves, people participate better in offering praise to God. Musicians will help if they truly practice the music for Mass and come prepared to lead.

Good preaching will help people realize the significance of their time together each Sunday. They will grow more aware of their faith and discover ways to put it into practice. Good worship will help Catholics become better Christians all week long, and their practice of the faith will enhance their worship.

17. May assemblies stand during the eucharistic prayer?

Assemblies do stand during the Preface and the Holy, Holy, Holy—which are part of the eucharistic prayer. In the United States the faithful kneel after the Holy, Holy, Holy until the prayer concludes.

There are exceptions when people are occasionally prevented by ill health, lack of space, the number of people present, or some other

In the dioceses of the United States, the assembly kneels during the eucharistic prayer after the Holy, Holy, Holy through the doxology and Amen.

reasonable cause. In those cases, they stand, but make a profound bow when the priest genuflects during the consecration.

In the early Church, it was quite common for people to stand throughout the eucharistic prayer. Standing is the default posture for Christian liturgical prayer because it puts the body in a position that anticipates the resurrection. The Eastern Churches all have the faithful stand throughout the eucharistic prayer.

In other parts of the Catholic world, people remain standing after the Holy, Holy, Holy until a little before the consecration. Then they stand up to sing the memorial acclamation. That is actually the default recommendation in the Vatican's universal legislation, which may be and has been amended in different ways by conferences of bishops.

18. Should presiders place a small crucifix upon the altar?

The *General Instruction of the Roman Missal* commends the use of images of the Lord, the Blessed Virgin Mary and the saints, but asks that their number not be increased indiscriminately.[164]

A crucifix is to be placed on or close to the altar.[165] In solemn celebrations, the priest incenses this crucifix when he incenses the altar both at the beginning of the celebration and during the preparation of the gifts. This helps unite the sacrifice of the Mass with the historic sacrifice of Christ on Calvary.

Some priests place an additional crucifix on the altar as a devotional item. In all Masses prior to the Second Vatican Council, the cross occupied a central place above the altar, serving as a visual focus for both priest and people. After the Council, the relative position between cross and altar became more varied; nonetheless, one crucifix was still required for the celebration of the Mass.

164. See GIRM, 318.
165. See GIRM 117 and 308.

A priest who sets a small crucifix on the altar so that he can see the image of Christ risks dividing the attention of the faithful between the two crosses, especially if they are looking over one in order to exchange dialogues with him during the eucharistic prayer. A better practice is for there to be one crucifix in relationship to the one altar. As the altar is not the priest's altar, but furniture belonging to the community, so the crucifix is not his alone, but belongs to the gathered people of God.

Still, a priest may argue that the extra cross helps him focus on the Mass, and therefore the duplication is not made "indiscriminately," but it is the kind of decision that can be confusing to the faithful.

19. How is the Ordo used?

The Ordo (Latin for *order*) is a liturgical almanac, published annually. You will need to use the Ordo that is specific to your diocese or religious community. The Ordo includes an entry for every day of the liturgical year, and includes all the information you need to prepare for the Mass. It tells you the liturgical color of the day, it explains where to find the readings and the presidential prayers, and includes notes about the Liturgy of the Hours. It also includes a variety of options—optional memorials of the saints, for example, as well as special observances like the World Day of Prayer for the Sick. Some Ordos include other useful information, like the pope's prayer intentions for each month, and the local necrology, that is, the list of names of deceased bishops and priests of your diocese. The shorthand the Ordo uses can take some getting used to, but once you get the hang of it you will find it an invaluable resource for preparing for the liturgy.

Here's a sample day from a typical Ordo, followed by an explanation of how to read it. Usually you'll find a key to the abbreviations at the beginning of the Ordo; you might even tear that page out and use it as a bookmark through the year, until you memorize the abbreviations.

Aug 9 Saturday: Weekday [18]; *Saint Teresa Benedicta of the Cross,*
m *virgin; martyr; BVM on Saturday*

Gr	HOURS	**Pss II** Seasonal wkdy *Sanctoral Common*
Rd		*of one martyr or of virgins Common of BVM on Sat*
Wh		EP I of Sun: begin **Pss II**
V^3R^3	MASS	any Mass *or of either mem*
	RDGS	412: Hb 1:12–2:4 Ps 9:8–13 Mt 17:14–20

The top line tells us the day and date: Saturday, August 9. It tells us that this is a weekday; and the number 18 in brackets tells us that we are in the Eighteenth Week in Ordinary Time. After that, in italics, we see that there are two optional memorials on this day. (Note that italics generally mean optional. The lowercase "m" in the left hand margin indicates that today's memorials are optional. On an obligatory memorial, feast, or solemnity, you would see a capital M, F, or S.) The first is the saint of the day, St. Teresa Benedicta of the Cross, or Edith Stein, the Carmelite martyr. The other optional memorial is the traditional remembrance of the Blessed Virgin Mary on Saturday. This means that the priest has some choices today. He can wear green and use the prayers and readings of the day (the ferial weekday). He can wear red and celebrate the memorial of St. Teresa Benedicta of the Cross, or he can wear white and offer Mass in honor of the Blessed Virgin Mary. (Note that the colors are indicated by the abbreviations Gr, Rd, and Wh on the left-hand margin. The fact that red and white are in italics indicates that they are optional.) It is good, if possible, to find out in advance which of the memorials—if any—the priest would like to celebrate.

The next three lines give us details about the celebration of the Liturgy of the Hours. "Pss II" means that we are in Week II of the four-week Psalter, and so we can simply turn to Saturday of Week II if we wish (the ferial weekday). The italics indicate other options—today, we can pray the office from the common of one martyr or of virgins in honor of St. Teresa, or we can pray the office from the Common of the Blessed Virgin Mary on Saturday. The next line tells us about Evening Prayer (EP), which on this Saturday evening anticipates the coming Sunday. In the Liturgy of the Hours, two offices of Evening Prayer are prayed each Sunday of the year, called "Evening Prayer I" and "Evening Prayer II." Evening Prayer I is prayed on Saturday evening, Evening Prayer II on Sunday Evening. With Evening Prayer I on Saturday evening, we begin a new week in the four-week Psalter. This example from the Ordo tells us to turn to Week III of the Psalter.

The next line takes us some of the options for the Mass. V^3, in the Ordo we are using as a sample, indicates that the priest may (in place of either the liturgy of the day or the optional memorials) choose a Votive Mass, a Ritual Mass, or one of the Masses for Various Needs and Occasions. R^3 means that funeral Masses as well as other Masses for the Dead are also permitted. Because this particular example from the Ordo is a day in Ordinary Time, the priest may choose "any Mass" as we see in the notations that follow. He can use any the prayers for the current week in Ordinary Time. Or he can select any of the prayers of Ordinary Time, the optional memorials of the day, or any Votive Mass, Ritual Mass, or Mass for Various Needs and Occasions. There are many options.

The final line in this entry in the Ordo gives us the readings of the day. The number "412" is the Lectionary number, and the full citations are included as well.

20. How do I mark *The Roman Missal*?

Your local Ordo will point you in the right direction. Let's take a couple of examples.

It's the Second Sunday of Advent. Use one ribbon to mark the "proper" prayers, that is, the prayers unique to this day in the liturgical calendar. You will find them at the beginning of *The Roman Missal*, in the Proper of Time. Use another ribbon to mark the Preface. You'll find the Prefaces in the center of *The Roman Missal* within the Order of Mass. There are two Advent Prefaces. Notice that the second is used only from December 17 to 24. That means you'll want to mark Preface I of Advent for today.

What else should be marked in *The Roman Missal*? It depends on local custom and the needs of the priest. It may be that another ribbon could be used to mark the Penitential Act for the day, either the Confiteor, or perhaps one of the sets of invocations found in Appendix VI. Some priests like to have the prayers for the preparation of the altar marked as well. You'll find those at the center of *The Roman Missal*, just after the Creed. (A helpful hint: fold the ribbons you are not using and tuck them out of sight, leaving visible only the ribbons that will be used during the current Mass. This will help prevent unnecessary flipping of pages.)

It's June 5, the memorial of St. Boniface. You find his prayers in Proper of Saints for June 5. But you notice right away that only one prayer, the Collect, is provided. So after you mark that page, you'll want to mark the rest of the prayers in one of the Commons. A note suggests using either the Common of Martyrs: For One Martyr or the Common of Pastors: For Missionaries, because St. Boniface was a missionary who carried the Gospel to the people of Germany. You might mark both of them, and let the priest decide which set he prefers.

Having marked the prayers, you next need to mark the Preface. Again, there are two options—you can mark one of the two Prefaces of Holy Martyrs or the Preface of Holy Pastors.

It's the Third Sunday of Lent, and the First Scrutiny of the Elect is being celebrated. There are two options for the prayers. You can mark the Prayers for the Third Sunday of Lent in the Proper of Time, or you can mark the prayers for the Scrutinies in the section Ritual Masses. Either set of prayers may be used when a Scrutiny is celebrated. Ask the priest which he prefers.

If the Scrutiny of the Elect is being celebrated in your parish, that means that the readings for Year A are being used as well. So you will want to mark the proper Preface for the Third Sunday of Lent, which is only used when the Gospel of the Woman of Samaria is read. Notice that this Preface is found in the Proper of Time, along with the other prayers for the Third Sunday of Lent. In Year B or Year C, when no Scrutiny is celebrated, one of the general Lenten Prefaces should be used. These are found in the Order of Mass.

21. How do I mark the Lectionary?

To mark the readings for a Sunday Mass, you need to know whether you are in Year A, Year B, or Year C. Here is a quick guide to the Lectionary for the next few years. Notice that the Lectionary year begins with the First Sunday of Advent, which usually falls in late November or very early December, and ends with the solemnity of Our Lord Jesus Christ, King of the Universe in late November of the following year.

	Sunday	**Weekday**
Advent 2019 – Christ the King 2020	Year A	II
Advent 2020 – Christ the King 2021	Year B	I
Advent 2021 – Christ the King 2022	Year C	II
Advent 2022 – Christ the King 2023	Year A	I

Once you know which year of the Lectionary you are in, it is easy to mark the Sunday Lectionary. You'll notice that every Sunday is assigned a distinctive number. This is very helpful as these numbers are unique to each set of readings. If the local Ordo tells you that the Sunday readings for today can be found at #60B, you'll find only one set of readings with that number no matter how many volumes of the Lectionary you thumb through — #60B refers to the readings for the Seventh Sunday of Easter in Year B.

After marking the Sunday Lectionary for the readers, you'll want to mark the Book of the Gospels for the deacon or priest. The number you used to find the readings in the Sunday Lectionary will help you find the appropriate Gospel as well.

It is helpful to place the Lectionary in a consistent place in the sacristy where the readers can review it before Mass. They will have prepared for their reading at home, but it is always good for them to see the words on the actual page they will be reading from. After the readers have had a chance to look at the Lectionary, the book can be placed at the ambo. The Book of the Gospels should similarly be placed where the priest or deacon can review the reading before Mass.

22. How do I prepare the vessels for Mass?

You have opened the church building, and prepared the vestments and books for the liturgy. Now you are ready to prepare the vessels for the celebration of the Mass. In the sacristy, you arrange the following items which will be placed on the credence table:

- the corporal to be placed on the altar at the Presentation and Preparation of the Gifts
- chalice, with a purificator
- the cruet containing water to be mingled with the wine
- the pitcher, basin, and towel for the washing of hands during the preparation of the gifts
- additional chalices, purificators, and ciboria for the distribution of Holy Communion to the assembly

In addition, you need to prepare the hosts and wine for the Mass. If there is to be a procession with the gifts, these will need to be placed on the offertory table in the nave when they are ready. How much to put out? Keep in mind that faithful should "receive the Lord's Body from hosts consecrated at the same Mass . . . "[166] A good way to ensure that this happens is to count the actual number in the assembly before preparing the hosts for Mass. The

166. GIRM, 85.

ushers can often help with this. If you put out the same number of hosts as there are people in the assembly (and don't forget to count the choir and the other ministers) you will be sure to have enough for everyone.

If hosts do need to be brought from the tabernacle, a minister may do it during the sign of peace. The ciborium can be placed on the altar and the priest can add hosts to the ciboria as well as from the hosts consecrated during the Mass. This is necessary at times, especially if there are many latecomers who were not factored into the count! This is also a good way to ensure that the hosts that are reserved in the tabernacle are kept fresh. However, it's always a good rule of thumb to include a little extra.

23. What kind of hosts and wine can be used in the liturgy?

"By reason of the sign, it is required that the material for the Eucharistic Celebration truly have the appearance of food" (GIRM, 321).

Hosts "must be made only from wheat, must be recently made, and, according to the ancient tradition of the Latin Church, must be unleavened."[167] The wine "must be from the fruit of the vine (cf. Lk 22:18), natural, and unadulterated, that is, without admixture of extraneous substances."[168] The bread and wine should also be fresh.[169] That means that leavened bread and fruit flavored wines may not be used for the Eucharist; nor is stale bread or wine that has turned to vinegar suitable for use in the Eucharist.[170]

The wine used should be of good quality, but there is no requirement that it be red, nor is there any specific indication as to its alcohol content. But it must be wine, not fruit juice. Priests and members of the assembly who are

167. GIRM, 320. See especially GIRM, 319–322.
168. GIRM, 322.
169. See GIRM, 323.
170. See Prot. 89/78–174, 98.

unable to drink alcohol can get permission from the Bishop to use mustum (grape juice without additives of any kind), for themselves only.

Another question that has come up recently is the idea of gluten-free hosts for people who are gluten intolerant. Because the hosts must be made of wheat, it is impossible to make an entirely gluten-free host. The Congregation of Benedictine Sisters of Perpetual Adoration in Clyde, Missouri, however, prepare very low-gluten hosts which have been deemed safe for those who suffer from gluten intolerance (see http://benedictinesisters.org/). Those who cannot receive even the small amount of gluten in such hosts can still receive Communion under the form of the Precious Blood. To read more about Celiac Sprue disease, visit the United States Conference of Catholic Bishops' Web site at www.usccb.org/liturgy/celiasprue.shtml.

24. What does it mean to purify vessels? Who may do this?

The vessels used to contain the consecrated bread and wine during the Mass receive a special cleansing called "purification" following Holy Communion or immediately following Mass. This purification stems from our Catholic belief in the real presence of Christ in Eucharist, and is carried out to ensure that any particles of the sacred species that may have remained in the paten or the chalice are reverently consumed. This rite of purification is carried out by a priest, deacon, or instituted acolyte.

Following Holy Communion or Mass, usually at the credence table, the paten and ciboria are carefully wiped over a chalice, so that any crumbs or fragments that remain can be collected. Any remaining Precious Blood is consumed, and then the chalices are rinsed with water (or with a mixture of wine and water, according to local custom), which the minister then consumes.

After this rite of purification, the vessels are ready to be cleaned by the sacristan or another minister: they are carefully rinsed in the sacrarium, and then washed and dried in the usual way.[171]

171. See GIRM, 278–280.

Appendix

Checklist for Participants

Here are some things that people can do to enhance their participation at Mass. You may wish to share these ideas with people who come to worship.

- **Prepare at home.** Develop a habit of daily prayer. Include some of the words of the Mass in your repertoire of prayer at home. These will help prepare you for Sunday worship with the community. Pay attention to the times that you sacrifice for others, and the times you rejoice with others as well.
- **Arrive on time.** Come to Mass on time, if not a little early. You can meet other people, catch up on their week, learn about their joys and struggles, and prepare yourself to worship as the Body of Christ. If you arrive late, you have not joined with others in the opening hymn. If you take your seat while the readings are being proclaimed, you will distract others from listening to the voice of God speaking to them. Arriving on time shows respect for others in the community, and to God who calls you together.
- **Greet the priest.** If your priest is standing by the door, say hello—before or after the Mass. But, if you have something important to tell him or discuss with him, be sure to contact him some other time instead. Standing at the door of the church and away from his office, vested for Mass, he is probably not able to make an appointment with you or even to remember an intention that's important to you. He really does care, but the number of people walking by is so large that he cannot remember everything people say to him before and after Mass. If you need to go to confession before Mass, try to go during the times your priest has already set aside. He may not be able to help you without prior notice in the precious minutes before Mass begins.
- **Sit in front.** You probably have a favorite place to sit. But if there are empty seats in front of you, move up. Participating at Mass demands your full attention. Nothing else should distract you. The closer you are to the action, the more easily and fully you will be able to participate.

- **Shut off electronic devices.** You may have a phone, a pager, a watch, or some other device that may create a sound or distract you with messages. You show respect for others in the assembly if you shut off these devices so as not to disturb their prayer. You will also concentrate better on the work you are now called to do.
- **Sing.** When you are invited to sing, do it. You will experience a deeper sense of prayer and a richer participation in the service. Your voice will blend with the voices of others, raising a chorus of praise to God. It will be beautiful for God to hear— but only if you sing.
- **Acknowledge your sins.** We all sin, and God loves us when we are honest about it. Your sins do not keep you from coming to Mass. Your humility helps you participate even better.
- **Pray.** When the priest says, "Let us pray," he means it. In the silence that follows those words, think hard about the reasons you are at Mass today, the intentions you hold in your heart. As you listen to the priest pray the Collect, find a place in it for the intentions you bring to Mass this day.
- **Listen to the readings.** When the readings are being proclaimed, listen intently. Put down the participation aids and anything else that may distract you. You are in God's house. God is speaking to you. Surely you want to listen. In the silence that follows each reading, think over the words that struck you and open your heart to them.
- **Pray for others.** In the universal prayer (the prayer of the faithful), you exercise your baptismal priesthood by praying for others. Think consciously of all those who need prayer around the world today.
- **Contribute to the collection.** Make an offering that will be included in the procession of the gifts. Your financial sacrifice signifies the offering you make of yourself. If you contribute nothing at all, you have to find other ways to join in the sacrifice of the Mass. Sadly, some people do not contribute money out of anger or frustration with something pertaining to the Church. Your offering does support the needs of your parish, but more importantly it is a sign of your sacrifice to God. If you withhold help from your parish at the collection, your sacrifice may appear stingy in the eyes of God. Give joyfully and generously, as Christ gave himself to you.
- **Thank God.** When the eucharistic prayer begins, the priest will recount many reasons for which we give God thanks. As he says, "Let us give

thanks to the Lord our God," think concretely about your reasons for giving God thanks today. Include these reasons in the Amen you sing at the end of the eucharistic prayer.

- **Adore Christ.** When the priest raises the host and the chalice during the eucharistic prayer, look up. Adore Christ who makes himself present to you.
- **Share peace.** Whenever you are invited to offer a sign of peace, share it with those nearby. Keep it focused on expressing the peace that is in your heart. This peace should help you prepare to receive Communion with others in the church.
- **Receive Communion.** Those invited to the supper of the Lamb are blessed, and that includes you. If for some reason you are ineligible for Communion, try to take care of it so that you may participate fully in the Mass.
- **Receive Communion from the cup.** When Communion from the cup is offered, you can experience a deeper participation in the eucharistic covenant that God made with us. At the Last Supper, Jesus invited the disciples to eat and drink. The same command applies to each of us. Eat his Body. Drink his Blood. This meal is the foretaste of the heavenly banquet. Experience the fullness of the presence of the Risen Christ under the form of wine.
- **Give thanks.** After receiving Communion, use the silence to thank God for the gift of the Eucharist. Be grateful that the Holy Spirit will help you this week through the grace of this sacrament.

Go. Stay for the end of Mass, and then go with other members of the community into the world to bring the Good News there. Don't leave early! If you leave after Communion, you avoid giving thanks to God for the Eucharist, hearing the announcements for activities during the week, receiving the blessing from the priest, and hearing the deacon's command to go as a body with him into the world. Christians have work to do. We love being at church. We love the Mass. We love being present with other members of the Body of Christ. But Christ expects more. He expects us to go. We never leave the Gospel behind. We take it with us. We never leave the community behind. We leave with them. We also take the fruits of this Eucharist, which we have faithfully celebrated in memory of Jesus.

Resources

Ritual Books

For the celebration of the Sunday Mass, parish liturgical staffs will need the following ritual books:

- *The Roman Missal*
- *Lectionary for Mass* (for Years A, B, or C)
- *Book of the Gospels*
- *Lectionary for Masses with Children* (for Years A, B, or C)
- *Eucharistic Prayers for Concelebration*
- *Eucharistic Prayer for Masses with Children*: Three Eucharistic prayers provided for use at Masses where preadolescent children make up the majority of participants. Although they do not appear in the third (current) edition of *The Roman Missal*, they have been adapted for use with the current edition and are published by the conferences of bishops of the United States and some other English-speaking countries
- *Sunday Celebrations in the Absence of a Priest*: Some parishes may not have a pastor and Sunday Mass may not be celebrated regularly. Instead, a lay leader of prayer might offer a Communion service with the celebration of a Liturgy of the Word or Liturgy of the Hours. In this situation, parish teams should use this ritual book.

For the official chants of the Mass, parish preparation teams may use the following:

- *Graduale Romanum: The Roman Gradual*, the liturgical book that contains the chants of the Mass, along with their musical notation. Both the ordinary and the proper of the Mass are contained in this book.
- *Graduale Simplex: The Simple Gradual*, a liturgical book that contains simpler chants to be sung in place of the more complex melodies found in the *Graduale Romanum*.

Ritual Masses may occur during the Sunday Mass. The ritual books for these rites include pastoral notes and ritual texts for when this happens. These rites include:

- *Rite of Christian Initiation of Adults*
- *Rite of Baptism for Children*
- *Order of Confirmation*
- *Order of Celebrating Matrimony*
- *Pastoral Care of the Sick: Rites of Anointing and Viaticum*
- *Book of Blessings*

Church Documents

In order for the Sunday Mass to be prepared carefully and according to the rubrics, parish preparation teams will need to be familiar with and regularly consult the following Church documents. Many of these documents can be found in LTP's The Liturgy Documents series (see especially volumes 1, 2, and 4). Many of these documents are referenced throughout this resource.

- *Built of Living Stones: Art, Architecture, and Worship*: A document from the United States Conference of Catholic Bishops, approved in 2000, that gives guidelines, norms, theological perspectives, and practical information for art, architecture, and furnishings in the building and renovating of churches in the United States. The document builds on and replaces its predecessor, *Environment and Art in Catholic Worship* (1978).
- *Ceremonial of Bishops* CB: The official book of directions and rubrics to aid bishops in celebrating the Mass, the sacraments, and other liturgies. The rubrics of the *Ceremonial of Bishops* are much more detailed than those in *The Roman Missal,* and thus the *Ceremonial of Bishops* is frequently an aid to understanding the rubrics in the Missal. The current edition was issued in 1984.
- *Circular Letter Concerning the Preparation and Celebration of the Easter Feasts*: A document issued by the Congregation for Divine Worship in 1988, also known by its Latin title *Paschale solemnitatis*, which contains norms, regulations, and various other pastoral and

doctrinal elements concerning Lent, Holy Week, the Sacred Paschal Triduum, and Easter Time.

- *Constitution on the Sacred Liturgy*: The first document of the Second Vatican Council, promulgated on December 4, 1963, also known by its Latin title, *Sacrosanctum Concilium*. It allowed the celebration of liturgical rites in the vernacular, called for the full, conscious, and active participation of the assembly, and ordered the revision of all liturgical rites. This is the foundational liturgical document for all other liturgical documents that have been issued since the Council and the lens through which liturgical law should be interpreted.
- *Directory on Popular Piety and the Liturgy*: A document issued by the Congregation for Divine Worship and the Discipline of the Sacraments in 2001 that discusses the proper relationship between the official liturgy of the Church and expressions of popular piety, offering both theological principles and practical guidelines.
- *Ecclesia de Eucharistia*: Encyclical of Pope John Paul II on the Eucharist and its relationship to the Church, issued April 17, 2003. In the letter, the pope sought to rekindle a sense of amazement as the Church recognizes the presence of Christ. Major sections of the letter deal with the Eucharist as the Mystery of Faith, how the Eucharist builds the Church, the apostolicity of the Eucharist and of the Church, the Eucharist and ecclesial communion, the dignity of the eucharistic celebration, and Mary as woman of the Eucharist.
- *General Instruction of the Roman Missal*: The introductory document that explains the theological background of and gives the directions for celebrating the Mass. It appears at the beginning of *The Roman Missal, and it is also published separately.*
- *Norms for the Distribution and Reception of Holy Communion under Both Kinds in the Dioceses of the United States of America*: Document issued by the United States Conference of Catholic Bishops and confirmed by the Apostolic See that gives norms for the administration of Communion under both kinds. It went into effect in 2002 and has the force of particular law for the Roman Catholic dioceses of the United States.
- *Redemptionis sacramentum*: The instruction on the Eucharist, on certain matters to be observed or to be avoided regarding the Most Holy Eucharist, issued in 2004 by the Congregation for Divine

Worship and the Discipline of the Sacraments. The document, which includes prescriptions of a juridical nature, addresses issues pertaining to the correct celebration of the Eucharist, noting some particular abuses and clarifying other proper procedures to be followed.

- *Sacramentum caritatis*: The postsynodal apostolic exhortation on the Eucharist as the source and summit of the Church's life and mission, issued by Pope Benedict XVI in 2007. The text discusses the relationship of the Eucharist to all the sacraments, the meaning of *ars celebrandi* (the art of celebration), the nature of participation at the celebration of the Eucharist, and connecting the Eucharist to the mission of living the Christian life.
- *Sing to the Lord: Music in Divine Worship*: Document issued by the United States Conference of Catholic Bishops, approved in 2007 and updated in 2012, that deals with music in Catholic worship. It addresses music as an integral part of liturgy and includes principles for the selection of appropriate music and specific questions concerning music in the rites of the Church. This document replaces the earlier documents *Music in Catholic Worship* and *Liturgical Music Today*.
- *Universal Norms on the Liturgical Year and the General Roman Calendar*: The document that outlines the regulations governing the celebrations of the liturgical year and the calendar for the universal Church. The liturgical days, their ranking, and the cycle of the year are all explained, and a table of liturgical days ranks the order of importance of the liturgical celebrations of the Church. It was promulgated by Pope Paul VI in 1969.

Theological and Historical Resources

- Bradshaw, Paul F., and Maxwell E. Johnson. *The Eucharistic Liturgies: Their Evolution and Interpretation*. Collegeville, MN: Pueblo, 2012. Coauthored by two superb scholars of the liturgy, this book presents a historical treatment of the evolution of eucharistic liturgies from their origins to the present day. Of interest to specialists in the field.

- Craig, Barry M. *Fractio Panis: A History of the Breaking of Bread in the Roman Rite.* Rome: Studia Anselmiana, 2011. Written by an Australian scholar of uncommon depth, this book treats the history of one part of the eucharistic liturgy: the breaking of bread.
- Foley, Edward. *From Age to Age: How Christians Have Celebrated the Eucharist.* Revised and expanded edition. Collegeville, MN: Liturgical Press, 2008. A much appreciated and much used resource, this book gives a comprehensive written and visual survey of the development of the Mass.
- Driscoll, Jeremy S., OSB. *What Happens at Mass.* Revised edition. Chicago: Liturgy Training Publications, 2011. This intelligent, straightforward guide to the Mass concentrates on the ritual form of the liturgy. Following the Order of Mass, Fr. Jeremy Driscoll explores the ways we proclaim the Resurrection of Jesus Christ by means of our words and ritual actions. Through our ritual celebration of the liturgy, this proclamation causes what once happened to be present now as the event happening at Mass, where the ritual forms of the bread, the wine, and the movements of the priest and people are all completely imbued with significance, with divine life itself.

Pastoral Resources

- Haas, David. *Music and the Mass: A Practical Guide for Ministers of Music.* Second edition. Chicago: Liturgy Training Publications, 2013. This resource provides a basic guide to key documents and principles regarding the celebration of the Eucharist. It walks through the Mass, rite-by-rite and step-by-step, describing each part through Scripture, Church documents, and various other sources. The author also offers commentary about the meaning of each part of the Mass through the lens of liturgical music. Music ministers will be inspired and grow in their faith as they learn more about the celebration of the Eucharist and how they contribute to the "joyful song of praise" that is the Mass.
- DeGrocco, Joseph. *A Pastoral Commentary on the General Instruction of the Roman Missal.* Chicago: Liturgy Training Publications, 2011. This is an accessible reference for priests and deacons, as well as all liturgical ministers and liturgy committees. It aims to help Catholics reflect more deeply on the meaning of the

Mass and the significance of what we do at Mass and aid parishes in celebrating the Eucharist in a way that is faithful to the norms of the Church and reflective of the goal of fully conscious and active participation envisioned by the *Constitution on the Sacred Liturgy.*

- Turner, Paul. *At the Supper of the Lamb: A Pastoral and Theological Commentary on the Mass.* Chicago: Liturgy Training Publications, 2011. This resource will help those who prepare the liturgy understand the parts of the Mass so they may enter them more intentionally and prepare for them. Following the Order of Mass at it appears in the third edition of *The Roman Missal*, this resource is an invitation to worship, a call to new intention, a deeper awareness of the privilege we share to be invited to the supper of the Lamb.
- Turner, Paul. *Let Us Pray: A Guide to the Rubrics of Sunday Mass.* Updated to conform to the revised English translation of *The Roman Missal.* Collegeville, MN: Pueblo, 2012. Collating the principle liturgical documents, this book walks the reader through the Mass from start to finish, showing what rubrics pertain to all the different parts. Both scholarly and pastoral, it is a user-friendly resource for those wondering what the rubrics say—and don't say.
- Turner, Paul. *My Sacrifice and Yours: Our Participation in the Eucharist.* Chicago: Liturgy Training Publications, 2013. In this short booklet, Paul Turner unpacks the meaning of the sacrifice of the Mass. In pastoral language, he explores more deeply how our participation in the Mass unites us to Christ. Through this guided reflection, we will become aware of the sacrifice Christ made for us, how we participate in this sacrifice each time we gather and participate in the eucharistic mystery, and how we give back as his disciples.
- Vanni, Trish Sullivan, Paul Turner, and Joyce Donahue. *From Mass to Mission: Understanding the Mass and Its Significance for Our Christian Life.* Chicago: Liturgy Training Publications, 2016. This series of booklets for adults, teens, and children provides a basic understanding of the Mass and our Christian call to discipleship. Individual leader booklets for adults, teens, and children.

Annual Publications

The following annual publications from Liturgy Training Publications will help you prepare and reflect upon the liturgy and ultimately live the call to "Go and announce the Gospel of the Lord."

- *At Home with the Word*
- *Celebrating Sunday for Catholic Families*
- *Children's Liturgy of the Word: A Weekly Resource*
- *Daily Prayer*
- *The Living Word: Sunday Gospel Reflections and Actions for Teens*
- *Sourcebook for Sundays, Seasons, and Weekdays*
- *Sunday Prayer for Catholics*
- *Workbook for Lectors, Readers, and Proclaimers of the Word*

The Liturgical Ministry Series

Those preparing liturgical ministers for the celebration of Sunday Mass might wish to refer to the following books in The Liturgical Ministry Series. Each book presents a theological and historical overview of the ministry with practical tips for best practice. Each volume is available in Spanish.

- *Guide for Cantors*, second edition, by Jennifer Kerr Breedlove and Paul Turner
- *Guide for Deacons* by Bob Puhala and Paul Turner
- *Guide for Extraordinary Ministers of Holy Communion* by Kenneth A. Riley and Paul Turner
- *Guide for Lectors* by Virginia Meagher and Paul Turner
- *Guide for Liturgy Committees by Paul Turner and Michael R. Prendergast*
- *Guide for Ministers of Liturgical Environment by Mary Patricia Storms and Paul Turner*
- *Guide for Ministers of Music*, second edition, by Jennifer Kerr Breedlove and Paul Turner
- *Guide for Sacristans*, second edition, by Corinna Laughlin and Paul Turner

- *Guide for Servers,* revised edition, by Corinna Laughlin, Robert D. Shadduck, Paul Turner, and D. Todd Williamson

Preparing Parish Worship™ Series

Each of the following books will help those who prepare the liturgy celebrate the sacramental rites at Sunday Mass. Following the same organizational structure, each book provides a theological and historical overview of the rite, guidance for best practice, answers to frequently asked questions, and a list of annotated resources and glossary definitions.

- *Guide for Celebrating Confirmation* by Paul Turner
- *Guide for Celebrating Christian Initiation with Adults* by Victorian M. Tufano, Paul Turner, and D. Todd Williamson
- *Guide for Celebrating Christian Initiation with Children* by Rita Burns Senseman, Victoria M. Tufano, and Paul Turner
- *Guide for Celebrating First Communion* by Jo-Ann Metzdorff and Paul Turner
- *Guide for Celebrating Infant Baptism* by Timothy Johnston, Paul Turner, and Paul Radkowski
- *Guide for Celebrating Matrimony* by Richard B. Hilgartner and Daniel J. Merz
- *Guide for Celebrating Worship of the Eucharist Outside Mass* by John Thomas Lane, sss

Glossary

Absolution: In the Mass, the words that conclude the penitential act, "May almighty God have mercy on us, forgive us our sins, and bring us to everlasting life," are called an absolution, but they are not sacramental in effect.

Acclamation: A brief, joyful liturgical response, such as "Amen" or "Blessed be God."

Acolyte: The liturgical minister charged with assisting the priest and deacon in the sanctuary. Although the title is frequently applied to any altar server, *acolyte* more specifically refers to a male for whom a bishop has included in the ritual celebration of the Institution of Acolytes, which is done almost exclusively for those preparing for ordination.

Alb: full-length white liturgical robe, from the Latin *albus*, meaning "white." The alb is the preferred vestment for all ministers, from server to bishop. It recalls the white garment first worn at Baptism as a sign of putting on the new life of Christ. Ordained ministers wear a stole and an outer garment over the alb.

Alleluia: Hebrew for "Praise the Lord"; an acclamation of praise. It is found in the Old Testament, particularly the psalms, and in the New Testament Book of Revelation. In some translations of the Bible it is found as "Hallelujah" or "Praise the Lord." In Roman Catholic liturgy it is used especially during Easter Time and omitted during Lent. At Mass it is sung before the proclamation of the Gospel.

Altar: The sacred table on which the sacrifice of the Mass is celebrated. It is the central symbol of Christ in a church building. In the United States, the table of the altar may be made of stone or wood; the base or supports may be made of any dignified and solid material. In new churches there is to be only one altar.

Altar Cloth: The cloth used to cover the altar during the celebration of Mass. One white cloth is required; additional cloths of other festive colors may be used provided the uppermost cloth covering the top of the altar is white.

Altar Cross: A cross with the figure of the crucified Christ on or near the altar during the celebration of Mass. If the processional cross bears a figure of the crucified Christ, it may serve as the altar cross.

Altar Server: The liturgical minister who assists the priest and deacon wat liturgies.

Ambo: The place from which all the Scripture readings are proclaimed and the homily may be preached during liturgy; a pulpit or lectern. The ambo is also used for the singing of the Exsultet, for announcing the intentions of the universal prayer, and for the leading of the responsorial psalm. The term is derived from a Greek word for "raised place."

Amen: Hebrew word meaning "so be it." It is a response of the assembly indicating agreement or assent. The concluding acclamation to the eucharistic prayer is commonly called the "Great Amen."

Antiphon: short refrain, frequently a verse of a psalm, used as a repeated congregational response to a psalm. At Mass, there is a suggested entrance antiphon and a Communion antiphon; the response of the responsorial psalm is also an antiphon.

Apostles' Creed: The ancient baptismal statement of the Church's faith. The questions used in the celebration of Baptism correspond to the statements of the Apostles' Creed. It may be used as the profession of faith at Mass and is particularly appropriate during Lent and Easter Time.

Asperges: The Latin term for the blessing and sprinkling of water.

Aspergil (Aspergillum): The liturgical object used to sprinkle holy water. It may be a metal wand-like instrument or a branch. Also called a sprinkler.

Aspersorium: The small bucket or vessel that holds holy water and that can be carried for the purpose of sprinkling the assembly.

Assembly: The people gathered for divine worship, often called the congregation.

Berekah: A Hebrew prayer form that blesses God, usually beginning with "Blessed are you, Lord our God, King of the universe." This is the basic style of the Hebrew grace after meals, the birkat ha-mazon, which seems to be the ancestor of the Christian eucharistic prayer.

Blessed Sacrament: The name commonly used to refer to the eucharistic bread after it has been consecrated.

Blessing: Any prayer that praises and thanks God. In particular, blessing describes those prayers in which God is praised because of some person or object, and thus the individual or object is seen to have become specially dedicated or sanctified because of the prayer of faith. Many blessing prayers ask God's favor toward a person in time of need or on a special occasion. Liturgical celebrations usually conclude with a blessing pronounced over the assembly.

Book of the Gospels: A ritual book from which the passages from the Gospel accounts prescribed for Masses on Sundays, solemnities, and feasts of the Lord are proclaimed. It is also called an evangeliary.

Breaking of Bread: The name by which the eucharistic liturgy was called in the apostolic Church, according to the Acts of the Apostles (2:42). Breaking bread is based on the biblical references to the action of Jesus at the Last Supper (Matthew 26:26, Luke 24:30, 35). It is also the term formerly used for the fraction of the bread at Mass.

Canon: An older name for Eucharistic Prayer I, especially the section after the Holy, Holy, Holy. The subtitle Roman Canon, which *The Roman Missal* assigns to Eucharistic Prayer I, reflects the older usage. It is Roman by origin, and it is a "canon" because for many centuries it was the only acceptable eucharistic prayer. It is therefore not correct to call other eucharistic prayers "canons".

Cantor: A liturgical minister who leads the singing of the assembly at a liturgy. The cantor may also sing alone, such as when singing the verses of the responsorial psalm, (when this minister may also be called a psalmist).

Catechumen: An unbaptized person who has declared their intention to prepare for the sacraments of initiation and has been accepted into the order of catechumens. Catechumens, though not yet fully initiated, are joined to the Church and are considered part of the household of Christ.

Celebrant: The presiding minister at worship. Hence, the presiding priest at Mass may be referred to as the celebrant. Use of the term in this sense must be balanced, however, by the emphasis in contemporary liturgical theology that all those in the liturgical assembly—priest and people alike—celebrate the Mass and together offer the sacrifice to God.

Celebrate: To enact a worship service—for example, "We celebrate Mass." The word is used both of the action of the priest or bishop, who may be said to "celebrate the Mass," and to the action of the entire assembly. While the common meaning of the term suggests a festive gathering, all liturgies, whether solemn or joyful, are called celebrations.

Censer: Another name for a thurible.

Chalice: The sacred vessel, usually a stemmed cup, used to hold the wine that is consecrated during the Mass.

Chalice Veil: A square cloth that may be draped over the chalice before it is brought to the altar for the Liturgy of the Eucharist. Its use is optional.

Chant: A sung text that is an integral part of the liturgy, such as the entrance chant and the communion chant. The term also refers to the actual singing of such texts.

Chasuble: The outer vestment of priests and bishops worn while celebrating the Eucharist. It is a large, sleeveless garment with a simple opening for the head worn over the stole and alb. The color of the chasuble matches that of the feast or liturgical time.

Ciborium: The liturgical vessel used for the eucharistic bread. Although many ciboria resemble chalices, contemporary ciboria are more commonly made in the form of bowls. Both styles frequently are made with a covering lid. The canopy or baldacchino over an altar is sometimes called a ciborium.

Collect: The opening prayer of the Mass. It sums up or collects the thoughts and prayers of the assembly, and concludes the Introductory Rites. After the collect, everyone is seated and the Liturgy of the Word begins. By tradition, the same prayer used as the collect of the Mass is also used as the concluding prayer for Morning Prayer and Evening Prayer in the Liturgy of the Hours.

Common: Term used for groups of texts in *The Roman Missal* and the *Liturgy of the Hours* that are used on feasts and memorials that do not have their own particular, or proper, texts assigned to them. Examples are the Common of the Blessed Virgin Mary, the Common of Martyrs, the Common of Pastors, and the Common of Holy Men and Women.

Communicant: A person who receives the Eucharist.

Communicantes: Name given to that paragraph in Eucharistic Prayer I that begins, "In communion with those whose memory we venerate." It expresses the assembly's union with the saints in the offering of the sacrifice. There are special forms of the Communicantes for the Nativity of the Lord and its octave, on the Epiphany of the Lord, at the Mass of the Lord's Supper, from the Easter Vigil until the Second Sunday of Easter, on the Ascension of the Lord, and on Pentecost Sunday.

Communion Antiphon: A verse from Sacred Scripture provided in *The Roman Missal* that may be sung or said during the reception of Holy Communion at Mass. Originally, the antiphon was the refrain from a psalm that was chanted during Holy Communion, which is still an option in the current Roman Missal.

Communion Rite: The portion of the Mass that begins immediately after the Amen of the eucharistic prayer and ends with the prayer after Communion. It includes the Lord's Prayer, the sign of peace, the fraction of the bread, and the reception of Holy Communion.

Concelebrant: A priest or bishop who celebrates Mass with other priests or bishops according to the norms for concelebration.

Concelebration: The form of the Mass in which several priests or bishops celebrate according to the norms for concelebration.

Concluding Rites: The last part of the Mass, following the Communion rite. It consists of brief announcements, a greeting, a blessing, and the dismissal of the assembly. If an additional rite follows the Mass, such as the final commendation at a funeral or a procession with the Blessed Sacrament, that rite replaces the Concluding Rites of the Mass. The term can also refer to the closing rites in any liturgy.

Confiteor: A common name given to the confession of sinfulness used in one form of the penitential act at Mass. The name is derived from the first word of the Latin version, *Confiteor Deo omnipotenti* ("I confess to almighty God").

Consecrate: To make holy and set apart through prayer. At Mass, the term refers to the sacramental action upon the bread and wine, which by consecration become the Body and Blood of Christ.

Consecration: That portion of the institution narrative in the eucharistic prayer when the priest pronounces the words of Christ at the Last Supper and the bread and wine are transformed into the Body and Blood of Christ.

Cope: A long, cape-like vestment. It may be worn in processions joined to a Mass (for example, the procession with palms on Palm Sunday) or at more solemn liturgical celebrations that occur outside Mass (for example, the Liturgy of the Hours or Benediction). The cope is normally worn only by an ordained minister.

Corporal: The cloth placed on the altar on which the vessels containing bread and wine are placed. It is traditionally square and is placed on top of the altar cloth. Its purpose is to designate the space for the offerings on the altar, and to catch any fragments of the Body and Blood of Christ that may fall.

Credence Table: The side table on which the vessels and articles needed for the celebration are placed when not in use, particularly during the celebration of the Eucharist.

Creed: Another name for the profession of faith, or symbol.

Cruet: A vessel, often a small pitcher, containing the wine or the water used in the celebration of the Eucharist.

Dalmatic: The sleeved outer vestment proper to a deacon, worn over the alb and stole. The color of the dalmatic matches the liturgical color of the feast or liturgical time. A bishop may wear one under his chasuble.

Dismissal: The final, formal invitation by the deacon or, in his absence, the priest, for the assembly to go forth from the liturgical celebration. The word can also refer to the dismissal of the catechumens after the homily at Mass, or of children for their own Liturgy of the Word.

Doxology: A hymn or prayer of praise to God. The Glory to God in the Highest, said or sung at Mass, is sometimes called the "Great Doxology," and the prayer "Glory to the Father, and to the Son, and to the Holy Spirit," used in the Rosary and the Liturgy of the Hours, is sometimes called the "Minor Doxology." Endings to certain prayers are also called doxologies if "praise" or "glory" are mentioned, such as the conclusion to the eucharistic prayer ("Through him, and with him, and in him . . . ") and the Lord's Prayer at Mass ("For the kingdom, the power and the glory are yours now and for ever").

Elements: A common term used to refer to the bread and the wine at Mass.

Elevation: The lifting up of the eucharistic bread and chalice during the celebration of Mass by the priest.

Embolism: An insertion of additional language into a text. It normally refers to the expansion of the Lord's Prayer during the Mass, "Deliver us, Lord, we pray, from every evil . . . " to which the people respond "For the kingdom, the power and the glory are yours now and for ever."

Entrance Antiphon: A text almost always taken from or based on Sacred Scripture that is sung or said at the very beginning of Mass, usually during the entrance procession. It is sometimes referred to as the introit or entrance chant. The entrance antiphon is given in *The Roman Missal.* Originally the antiphon began and concluded a psalm that was chanted during the entrance, which is still an option in the current Missal.

Entrance Procession: The formal liturgical movement of the priest and ministers to the sanctuary at the beginning of Mass.

Epiclesis: Greek word derived from the verb "to call upon" or "to invoke." Epiclesis can refer to any petition or request, but it is most commonly used to refer to the section of the eucharistic prayer that asks the Holy Spirit to come upon the bread and wine.

Eucharist: The sacrament whereby Christ becomes truly, completely, and permanently present under the appearances of bread and wine. The entire action of celebrating the sacrifice of the Mass is commonly called the Eucharist, as are the consecrated elements. The word is derived from the Greek for "thanksgiving"; it was used as early as the *Didache* and St. Justin (c. 100–c. 165).

Eucharistic Prayer: The central prayer of the Mass. It is an act of thanksgiving, praise, blessing, and consecration. It corresponds to Jesus' act of blessing during the Last Supper, the second of the fourfold actions of taking, blessing, breaking, and giving by which the Eucharist is often described. The eucharistic prayer includes the form of the sacrament; the words of Christ ("This is my Body . . . this is the chalice of my Blood . . . ") are essential. In Greek-speaking churches it is called the anaphora. Scholars suggest that the eucharistic prayer may have developed from the *birkat ha-mazon,* the Jewish grace after meals.

The eucharistic prayer includes a thanksgiving to God for the work of salvation, an acclamation (the Sanctus), an epiclesis, the institution narrative and consecration, the anamnesis, the oblation or offering of the memorial to God, together with the sacrifice of the assembly, the intercessions, prayers for the whole Church, and the final doxology.

Eucharistic Reservation: The practice of keeping the bread of the Eucharist in the tabernacle. The primary and original reason for reservation is the administration of Viaticum; it is also for the adoration of our Lord and for the giving of Holy Communion outside Mass, particularly to the sick and homebound. The practice stems from the Catholic belief that the Real Presence of the Lord remains permanently after consecration.

Eucharistic Sacrifice: The Mass

Eucharistic Species: One or both of the elements of bread and wine that have been consecrated and have become the Body and Blood of Christ.

Extraordinary Form of the Mass: The Mass celebrated according to *The Roman Missal* promulgated after the Council of Trent as updated in 1962 by Pope John XXIII; sometimes referred to as the Tridentine Mass. The term originated with Pope Benedict XVI in his 2007 apostolic letter *Summorum pontificum*. The term distinguishes this celebration of the Mass from the ordinary form.

Extraordinary Minister of Holy Communion: The liturgical minister who is authorized by the bishop to assist priests and deacons in the distribution of Holy Communion. An extraordinary minister functions when a sufficient number of ordinary ministers is not present.

Feast: A rank within the category of liturgical days, lower than a solemnity but higher than a memorial. Feasts usually do not include Evening Prayer I, but usually do have a complete proper set of texts for the Mass along with readings.

Feria: The Latin word for "weekday." It refers to a day on which there is no solemnity, feast, or obligatory memorial assigned.

Final Blessing: A blessing given at the conclusion of a liturgy. It may take the form of a simple blessing, a solemn blessing, or a prayer over the people.

First Reading: The first Scripture reading during the Liturgy of the Word. On Sundays and other important days, it is usually taken from the Old Testament, or, during Easter Time, from the Acts of the Apostles or Revelation. On weekdays, it may be taken from either the Old Testament or the New Testament writings of the Apostles, but not from the Gospel accounts.

Flagon: A pitcher that may be used to hold the wine that is carried forward in the procession with the gifts. Ideally, it is large enough to hold all the wine to be consecrated as a sign of the assembly's unity in the eucharistic celebration. The wine is to be poured from the flagon into chalices during the preparation of the gifts.

Fraction of the Bread: The ritual action of dividing the common loaf of eucharistic bread into many pieces to be distributed at Holy Communion. In the Roman Rite this takes place after the recitation of the Lord's Prayer and the sign of peace, and before the invitation to participate in Holy Communion. It signifies that the many faithful are made one body by partaking of the one loaf.

Gift Table: The table located in the midst of the assembly on which the gifts of bread and wine are placed before they are carried in procession to the altar at the beginning of the Liturgy of the Eucharist.

Gifts: The elements of bread and wine to be consecrated to become the Body and Blood of Christ. After the preparation of the gifts, these same elements are called the offerings.

Gloria in Excelsis: The song of praise, which in English begins with the words "Glory to God in the highest," sung on certain prescribed days as part of the Introductory Rites of the Mass. Its opening line is based on the hymn of the angels at Christ's birth (see Luke 2:14).

Gospel: The Good News of Jesus Christ. The term *Gospel* usually refers to one of the four accounts of the life, death, and Resurrection of Jesus found in the Bible, ascribed to Matthew, Mark, Luke, and John.

Gospel Acclamation: The title given to the rite within the celebration of Mass that greets the Lord who is about to speak to the assembly in the Gospel and prepares the assembly for its proclamation. The Gospel acclamation consists of the Alleluia (or, during Lent, other words of praise) sung by all, followed by a verse (frequently from Scripture) sung by a cantor or by the choir, and then the refrain sung again by all. In practice, several verses may be used to cover the action of a lengthy Gospel procession.

Gospel Procession: The name for the procession of the deacon or priest to the ambo for the proclamation of the Gospel. The minister takes the *Book of the Gospels* and processes with it from the altar to the ambo during the singing of the Gospel acclamation. He may be preceded by a thurifer and/or by ministers with candles.

Greeter: A liturgical minister who welcomes individuals as they arrive at a church for worship. In many parishes, ushers also perform the ministry of greeter. Sometimes they are referred to as ministers of hospitality.

Greeting: A brief, formalized dialogue using ritual language usually expressing a wish for God's grace or presence to another, including a standardized response by the one(s) being greeted, for example, "The grace of our Lord Jesus Christ, and the love of God, and the communion of the Holy Spirit be with you all" to which the people respond with the words, "And with your spirit." The liturgical greeting should not be replaced or embellished with secular greetings such as "Good morning" since it is ritual language seeking the presence of God.

Holy, Holy, Holy: The English name for the Sanctus—that is, the preface acclamation which forms part of the eucharistic prayer and begins with the words, "Holy, Holy, Holy Lord God of hosts."

Homily: An exhortation based on the Scripture readings or other text from the Mass being celebrated, usually after the proclamation of the Gospel. It reflects on the implications of Scripture and challenges the assembly to conversion and renewal. The homily at Mass is reserved to the ordained. At Mass, the homily is ordinarily given by the celebrant, although it may be entrusted to a concelebrating priest or to the deacon. A homily is integrally related to the liturgy being celebrated. It differs from a sermon, which is a thematic talk not necessarily related to the liturgical action or texts.

Institution Narrative: The section of the eucharistic prayer in which the celebrant narrates to the Father what the Lord Jesus did and said at the Last Supper when he instituted the Eucharist. The traditional Catholic teaching is that when the priest repeats the words of Christ during this section of the eucharistic prayer, the bread and wine are consecrated and become the Body and Blood of Christ. Thus the institution narrative is sometimes referred to as the "words of institution" or the "consecration."

Intinction: The form of distributing Holy Communion under both kinds in which a priest dips a particle of the consecrated bread into a chalice containing the consecrated wine and places it directly into the communicant's mouth. Reception of Holy Communion in the hand is not permitted when intinction is used. Although allowed by law, it is a less preferred manner for distributing Holy Communion since the sign value of drinking from the chalice in obedience to the Lord's command has been eliminated.

Introductory Dialogue: The first six lines of the eucharistic prayer spoken in dialogue between the celebrant and the people. "**V**. The Lord be with you. **R**. And with your spirit. **V**. Lift up your hearts. **R**. We lift them up to the Lord. **V.** Let us give thanks to the Lord our God. **R**. It is right and just."

It is a very ancient part of the eucharistic prayer dating to at least the third century.

Introductory Rites: The beginning of Mass or another liturgy. The Introductory Rites at Mass usually consist of the entrance procession, the sign of the cross, the greeting, the penitential act or rite of sprinkling, the Gloria, when prescribed, and the collect.

Introit: The entrance antiphon. In the Tridentine Missal the complete introit consists of the antiphon, a psalm verse, the Glory to the Father, and a repetition of the antiphon. Except for the Glory to the Father, the same pattern is found in the post–Vatican II *Graduale Romanum*.

Kyrie: Vocative case of *kyrios*, a Greek word meaning "lord" or "master." In the liturgy, "Kyrie, eleison" may have originally been the response to a litany similar to the present Universal Prayer. It now forms a short litany addressed to Christ that is part of the Introductory Rites of the Mass.

Lamb of God: The English name for the Latin *Agnus Dei*, a litany sung during the breaking of the bread during the fraction rite at Mass. The term is sometimes imprecisely used to refer to the fraction rite itself.

Latin: The language traditionally used in worship by the Roman Rite of the Catholic Church. Liturgical books are first issued in Latin (typical editions) and then translated into other languages.

Lavabo: A name sometimes used to refer to the washing of hands at Mass. It is derived from Psalm 26:6—"*Lavabo inter innocents manus meas: et circumdabo altare tuum, Domine*" ("I wash my hands in innocence and take my place around your altar"). In the Tridentine Missal this psalm is said quietly by the priest during the washing. The revised Missal uses a different text, taken from Psalm 51, but the older name for this action continues to be used.

Lavabo Bowl: The bowl used at the washing of hands at Mass.

Lay Faithful: All the baptized except those who are ordained.

Lay Minister: A member of the lay faithful who performs a designated liturgical action at Mass or other liturgy.

Lector: The liturgical minister who proclaims the biblical readings (except the Gospel) at liturgies. Although the title is frequently applied to any reader, *lector* more specifically refers to a male whom a bishop has included in the Institution of Lectors, which is done almost exclusively for those preparing for ordination. Such ministers are called *instituted lectors*.

Liturgical Calendar: A listing of dates of the year with the corresponding liturgical celebrations held on those dates. The General Roman Calendar, the basic calendar for the Roman Catholic Church, is found in the front of *The Roman Missal*. Nations, regions, dioceses, and religious institutes may have their own particular calendars, which supplement the general calendar.

Liturgical Year: The annual cycle of liturgical celebrations, centered on the celebration of Easter.

Liturgy: Any official form of public worship, from the Greek word *leitourgia*, "work of the people." In the Eastern Churches, the Mass is often called the Divine Liturgy. The title is frequently used in conjunction with a modifier, such as the Liturgy of the Hours or the Liturgy of the Eucharist. "The liturgy" is often used to refer to the Mass.

Liturgy Committee: A body of people charged with assisting the pastor, the liturgy director, other pastoral leadership, and the assembly in preparing for and enacting liturgical celebrations. Members of any liturgy committee should be properly formed to understand the Church's tradition and what is proper in the celebration of the sacred Liturgy.

Liturgy of the Eucharist: One of two major sections of the Mass, along with the Liturgy of the Word. It begins after the universal prayer and ends with the prayer after Communion. It is structured around the fourfold eucharistic actions of "take, bless, break, give," enacted in the presentation and preparation of the gifts, the eucharistic prayer, the fraction rite, and the Communion rite.

Liturgy of the Word: One of two major sections of the Mass, along with the Liturgy of the Eucharist. It follows the Introductory Rites and ends with the universal prayer.

Lord's Day: Another name for Sunday. It was used as early as the first century, in the Acts of the Apostles and the *Didache*.

Mass: The name for the entire celebration of the Eucharist of the Roman Rite. It is derived from the Latin word for "dismissal," *missa,* and therefore implies the mission of those who have participated in it.

Memorial: (1) A common way of translating the word *anamnesis* and of understanding the concept. In liturgical theology, however, anamnesis is not understood as a memorial ceremony that merely recalls a past event. It is understood, rather, as the active remembrance and making present of a saving reality. (2) The rank of liturgical days lower than both solemnities and feasts. Memorials may be classified as either obligatory or optional.

Memorial Acclamation: The acclamation made by the assembly during the eucharistic prayer, after the institution narrative and the declaration, "The mystery of faith." Three possible texts are given in *The Roman Missal.* Each acclamation addresses Christ and refers in some way to the complete Paschal Mystery, including his second coming.

Mustum: Fresh grape juice that has just begun the fermentation process. The bishop may permit the use of mustum in place of or in addition to wine at Mass for situations such as when a priest or a member of the lay faithful cannot tolerate alcohol.

Oblation: The act of offering. The term is also used for the offerings of bread and wine at Mass.

Obligatory Memorial: A liturgical day with the rank of memorial. On such a day, the Mass of the memorial is to be used, rather than the weekday Mass of the current liturgical time. The word *obligatory* does not appear in the missal's Proper of Saints, but its meaning is implied with every *memorial.* Contrasts with *optional memorial.*

Offerings: (1) The gifts of bread and wine. They symbolize the offering of self that each member of the assembly makes together with Christ's offering of himself to God the Father. (2) The term *offering* is sometimes used for the monetary donation in the collection, and in the sum that an individual gives to a priest as a stipend to remember a particular intention at a Mass.

Optional Memorial: A liturgical day that may be observed with the rank of memorial. On such a day, the Mass of the memorial may be used but is not obligatory. Another Mass, even the weekday Mass of the current liturgical time, may be celebrated.

Orans Position: A posture of prayer in which the arms are uplifted toward heaven, stretched out slightly forward, with palms upward. Many old icons depict the saints in prayer with arms in this position. It is the position used by the presiding priest when saying the presidential prayers at liturgy—for example, the orations at Mass.

Ordinary Form of the Mass: The Mass celebrated according to the post–Vatican II Order of Mass promulgated in 1969 by Pope Paul VI and reissued in the third typical edition of *The Roman Missal* by Pope John Paul II in 2000. This Mass reflects the reform of the liturgy that was undertaken after the Second Vatican Council. The term distinguishes this form of the Mass from the extraordinary form.

Ordo: (1) A term used for the order or ordinary of the Mass, especially used of the Roman *ordines*, documents that described the early Roman liturgies. (2) A term that can be to designate groups of rites, as in the title *Order of Christian Funerals.* (3) The detailed annual liturgical calendar that indicates which liturgical celebrations occur on which days, and which texts may or must be used in the celebration of Mass and of the Liturgy of the Hours on a specific day.

Paten: The name for the plate which holds the eucharistic bread during Mass. Although the term is associated with a small, disk-like plate sized to hold only one large host for the priest, it can also be applied to a larger plate containing a sufficient amount of bread for the communion of the entire assembly. It is preferable to use only one large plate as a sign of the unity of the assembly and the offering of one sacrifice. A large paten would still be distinguished from a ciborium, however, in that a paten more resembles a plate, dish, or tray, whereas a ciborium resembles a cup or a bowl with a lid.

Penitential Act: The short ritual expression of sinfulness that normally takes place as part of the Introductory Rites of the Mass. The rite has three options: the first is a confession, usually called the Confiteor, recited by the priest and the assembly together; the second option consists of two psalm verses said by the priest with responses by the assembly; and the third option incorporates the Kyrie into spoken or sung invocations to Christ. It is omitted whenever the rite of blessing and sprinkling water takes place, when another liturgical action is joined to the beginning of Mass (such as the reception of children for Baptism), and on Ash Wednesday.

Praenotanda: An introductory text in a ritual book. It provides important theological foundations and explanations for the ritual, along with norms, rubrics, and other instructions. Sometimes it is replaced with a longer document, such as the *General Instruction of the Roman Missal.*

Prayer after Communion: One of the presidential prayers in the Mass. It is said after the distribution of Holy Communion and the period of silence or hymn of praise that follows, concluding the Liturgy of the Eucharist. The announcements and other elements of the Concluding Rites follow the prayer after Communion.

Prayer over the Offerings: One of the presidential prayers in the Mass. It is said at the conclusion of the preparation of the gifts and immediately precedes the eucharistic prayer.

Prayer over the People: A prayer of blessing addressed to God that may immediately precede an expanded formula of blessing at the end of Mass. *The Roman Missal* contains prayers over the people for Ash Wednesday and the Sundays of Lent, optional texts for other weekdays of Lent, and forms for general use throughout the liturgical year and on the feasts of saints, which may be used at the discretion of the presider.

Preface: The first section of the eucharistic prayer, starting with the introductory dialogue and ending with the Sanctus (Holy, Holy, Holy). It proclaims the motives for giving thanks to God in this particular celebration, and therefore it is often proper to a particular liturgical season or day. The name is derived from a Latin word for "proclamation." It is part of the eucharistic prayer, not an introduction to it, as its name in English might suggest.

Preparation of the Gifts: The first section of the Liturgy of the Eucharist, during which the altar is prepared with the items that will be needed for that part of the Mass; sometimes referred to as the offertory, from its name in the Tridentine Missal, and the name still used for the chant that may be sung at this time. It begins with the bread and wine being brought in procession to the altar. The priest prepares the gifts with the prescribed prayers, washes his hands, and prays the prayer over the offerings, which concludes the rite.

Presidential Prayers: The prayers that the priest celebrant prays audibly in the name of the entire assembly.

Presidential Chair: The chair used by the presiding priest at a liturgy. It signifies "his function of presiding over the gathering and of directing the prayer."[172]

172 GIRM, 31.

Profession of Faith: The formula that expresses what the Church believes about God. It is also referred to as the "symbol" or the "creed."

Progressive Solemnity: The principle that may guide the choices concerning what should be sung in a liturgy. In the fullest, most solemn form, everything that demands singing would be sung; the simplest form would involve no singing at all. In between are various degrees of how much will be sung, stemming from the nature of the celebration. Considerations regarding the degree of solemnity include the time of the liturgical year, the day of the week, and the rank of the day on which the celebration takes place. Other considerations include the nature and style of the music, the use of various instruments, and which parts of the rite will be sung.

Profound Bow: A bow of the body; a bow from the waist. This type of bow is made to the altar by the ministers in the procession at the beginning and end of Mass and in general whenever anyone in the liturgical assembly passes in front of the altar. Everyone in the liturgical assembly makes a profound bow during the creed in recognition of the Incarnation, and during prayers over the people and solemn blessings at the end of the Mass. There are also prescribed times in the liturgy when the priest and the deacon make profound bows.

Proper: Those texts in the Mass and in the Liturgy of the Hours that are particular to a given day. The complete proper for Mass includes the entrance antiphon, communion antiphon, readings, orations, and preface. The proper is distinguished from the ordinary and the common.

Purification (Purify): The cleansing of liturgical vessels to remove any trace of the consecrated eucharistic elements; formerly called the ablutions. This cleansing may be performed by a priest, deacon, or instituted acolyte after Communion or after Mass. This cleansing is different from the ordinary washing of vessels for cleanliness, which takes place after Mass, after the purification is completed.

Purificator: The cloth used to wipe the rim of the chalice containing the Blood of Christ after someone drinks from it during the celebration of the Eucharist.

Responses: The answers made by the assembly to the various prayers and dialogues during the celebration of any liturgy.

Responsorial Psalm: The psalm or canticle that is sung or recited after the first reading in a liturgy. It is normally proclaimed responsorially: a psalmist sings the text of the psalm and the assembly sings a response usually taken from a verse of the same psalm.

Roman Canon: The name given to Eucharistic Prayer I in *The Roman Missal.* It was the only eucharistic prayer (with minor changes) used in the Roman Church before the Second Vatican Council since at least around the time of Pope Gregory the Great (590–604).

Rubric: A direction or explanatory instruction printed between prayers or other spoken texts of a liturgical rite. The word *rubric is derived from the* Latin word for "red" because rubrics are normally printed in red in the liturgical books. Some rubrics are descriptive, and thus may be adapted in certain situations; others are prescriptive, and thus must be carried out as written. Rubrics are meant to give structure and order to a ritual. The term is often used in the plural to speak of the norms or directives of a liturgy as a whole.

Sacristan: The liturgical minister who has the responsibility for preparing everything needed for liturgical celebrations.

Sacrarium: A special sink, usually with an attached cover, whose drain goes directly into the ground rather than into a sewer, found in the sacristy of a church. Its purpose is primarily the disposal of water used for cleansing the sacred vessels and other items that come in contact with the eucharistic elements.

Sacristy: The room in which vestments and liturgical items are stored and prepared for use before liturgies. It is also commonly used as a vesting room, although larger churches and cathedrals may have a separate vesting room, called the secretarium.

Sanctuary: The area of the church in which the presidential chair, altar, and ambo are located, and in which the primary ministers may also sit. Normally it is somewhat elevated, for the sake of visibility. It should be in some way distinct from the other areas of the church, yet at the same time integrally related to the entire space, to convey a sense of unity and wholeness. It is sometimes referred to as the presbyterium or chancel.

Sanctuary Lamp (or Light, or Candle): The flame required to be kept burning near the tabernacle when the Blessed Sacrament is reserved, as a sign of honor for the presence of Christ. The lamp is to be either of oil or of wax.

Second Reading: On Sundays and certain major celebrations, a second reading is proclaimed after the first reading and the responsorial psalm. It is taken from one of the books of the New Testament other than the Gospel accounts.

Sequence: A poetic hymn sung before the Gospel acclamation on certain days. Sequences are required on Easter Sunday and Pentecost; they are optional on the Solemnity of the Most Holy Body and Blood of the Lord and on the Memorial of Our Lady of Sorrows.

Sign of Peace: The ritual greeting that may take place during the Liturgy of the Eucharist, before the fraction rite. The actual sign that is exchanged (for example, a handshake, a hug, a bow, a kiss) will vary greatly from assembly to assembly, and even at times from person to person, and reflects the culture of the people.

Solemn Blessing: The form of blessing in which the standard Trinitarian formula is usually preceded by three invocations. The assembly responds to each of these invocations with "Amen." Formulas for solemn blessings to be used at Mass are given in *The Roman Missal.*

Solemnity: A category of liturgical day that is higher than a feast or a memorial. The celebration of a solemnity begins with Evening Prayer I on the preceding day. Some solemnities also have their own Vigil Mass, to be used on the evening of the preceding day if Mass is celebrated at that time.

Species: One or both of the consecrated elements of bread and wine that have become the Body and Blood of Christ. The term is usually *sacred species* when referring to the consecrated elements.

Stole: The vestment worn over the neck by ordained ministers. It is a long band of fabric about five inches wide. A priest or bishop wears the stole around the neck and hanging down in front. A deacon wears the stole over the left shoulder and fastened at his waist on the right side. At Mass, the stole is worn underneath the chasuble or dalmatic.

Sunday: The weekly commemoration of the Lord's Resurrection. It is both the first day of the week and also the eighth day. It is also called the Lord's Day. Sunday is the original feast day and the preeminent day for the Church to gather for liturgy.

Tabernacle: The safe-like receptacle for storing the consecrated eucharistic bread. When the Blessed Sacrament is present in the tabernacle, it is to be locked and the sanctuary light set aflame. The tabernacle must be immovable, solid, and not transparent.

Thurible: A vessel in which incense is burned on coals; also called a censer. Originally, thuribles were either open bowls, or braziers, that remained stationary. Modern thuribles are usually metal vessels with pierced lids that allow air to keep the coals alight. They are suspended by one or more chains and, in the Roman Rite, held midway along the chains while swung toward the object or person being reverenced. In the Eastern Rites, the censer is usually swung at the full-length of the chains.

Thurifer: The liturgical minister who carries and swings the thurible during liturgies; also called a censer bearer. As a ministerial role, it is assigned to an instituted acolyte or other altar server.

Universal Prayer: The intercessory prayers in the celebration of the Mass, following the creed on Sundays and solemnities or the homily on other days; also called the "prayer of the faithful" or "bidding prayers," and formerly called the "general intercessions." It consists of an introduction, intentions and responses to the intentions, and a concluding prayer.

Usher: The liturgical minister who helps seat people as they arrive at the church for worship, who takes up the collection, and who helps organize and direct processions of the faithful, such as the procession with the gifts and the Communion procession. An usher may also fulfill the ministry of greeter.

Vestments: The ritual garments and symbols of office worn by various ministers at liturgy.